Chapter

The Warrior Mindset

Embracing Challenges and Transforming Your Life

Introduction to the Warrior Mindset

Welcome to your journey.
I want to share with you a powerful concept that has been a driving force in my life and has the potential to transform yours as well - the warrior mindset. "What is the warrior mindset?" It's a mental framework that embodies resilience, determination, adaptability, and unwavering focus. It's the mindset that enables us to face challenges head-on, turn obstacles into opportunities, and strive for personal growth. The warrior mindset isn't about becoming invincible or fearless - it's learning to dance with fear and uncertainty. I found myself at a crossroads. I faced the decision to leave a stable corporate job to venture into the unknown world of entrepreneurship.
The risks were high, the uncertainties, and yes, there was plenty of self-doubt. But here's where the warrior mindset came into play. Instead of succumbing to fear and sticking with the familiar, I embraced the challenge. I set clear goals, developed a strategic plan, and put in the hours, days, and years to build my business from scratch. It was far from easy, there were inevitable setbacks and failures, but the warrior mindset kept me going. It gave me the resilience to bounce back from the losses and the determination to keep moving forward, no matter how tough things got. That is just one example of where I have applied the warrior mindset in real life, and through this book, we'll explore many more. This book isn't just my story. This book is a journey of personal growth, transformation, and empowerment. I'm here to guide you, share the strategies, and help you unlock your inner warrior. The path won't require commitment, courage, and hard work. But trust me. The rewards are worth every challenge.

Defining the Core Qualities of the Warrior Mindset

The warrior mindset isn't just about battling life's obstacles - it's about how we approach our daily lives, goals, and relationships. It's about the internal qualities that help us survive and thrive in a world of challenges and opportunities. Let's take a moment to define some of these core qualities:

1. Resilience is the ability to weather the storms of life and come back stronger. It's not avoiding failures or setbacks - warriors often invite these opportunities for learning and growth. When I embarked on my entrepreneurship journey, resilience was the buoy that kept me afloat amid uncertainty and challenges.
2. Determination is about having a clear vision of what you want and committing to it, no matter the obstacles. It's the driving force that keeps you moving forward, even when the road ahead seems long and arduous. My determination to build a successful business remained strong despite my hurdles.
3. Adaptability is the capacity to adjust to new conditions and to be flexible in the face of change. In today's fast-paced world, the only constant is change. By learning to be adaptable, I could pivot my strategies when needed, always aligning my actions with the current reality rather than sticking to an outdated plan.
4. Focus is the ability to direct your attention and energy towards a specific goal without getting distracted by the noise around you. Focus can be a challenging trait to develop in an age of constant distractions. Still, it's crucial for achieving any form of lasting success. My ability to stay focused on my goal, despite various distractions and demands was pivotal to my entrepreneurial journey.

These qualities form the pillars of the warrior mindset. Honing these skills takes time and practice. They are not inherent traits that you're either born with or not - that's the beauty of it. The warrior mindset is accessible to everyone. No matter where you are in your life right now, no matter your past experiences or future ambitions, you have the potential to cultivate these qualities and harness their power. In the following chapters, we'll delve deeper into these core qualities. We'll explore practical strategies, share insights from scientific research, and provide real-life examples to help you develop and strengthen these skills. Together, we'll embark on this journey to unlock your inner warrior and empower you to conquer challenges, achieve your goals, and transform your life. Are you ready? Let's march forward.

The Importance of Ownership and Responsibility

The warrior mindset is not just about resilience, determination, adaptability, and focus. At its core, it's about taking full ownership and responsibility for your life, actions, and choices. It means acknowledging that you are the sole author of your life story and that your decisions and actions shape your journey and future.
When I made the leap from a secure corporate job to entrepreneurship, I took complete ownership of that decision. I knew the risks involved, the potential pitfalls, and the challenges that lay ahead. But I also recognised the potential rewards and the opportunity to create something of my own. Taking ownership meant not blaming circumstances or external factors for my setbacks. When things didn't go as planned, I didn't point fingers at market conditions or my competition. Instead, I looked inward, reflecting on my strategies, decisions, and the areas I could improve. The journey is a challenging path to tread. It's always simpler to

attribute our difficulties to external forces, to circumstances beyond our control is always simpler. However, when we give away that power, we also give away our ability to create change. We limit our potential for growth and transformation. The warrior mindset encourages us to embrace responsibility. It empowers us to say, "I am in control. I am responsible for my successes and my failures. And if something needs to change, it's up to me. Taking responsibility fosters resilience and determination. It cultivates adaptability because it encourages us to learn from our experiences to adjust our sails based on the winds of our lives. And it enhances our focus, directing our energy towards our goals and actions instead of external factors we cannot control. As we progress in this book, I want you to remember the power of ownership and responsibility. Embrace, welcome, and let it guide you to unleash your inner warrior.

Creating Positive Change through the Warrior Mindset

Its transformative potential sets the warrior mindset apart from other ways of thinking. This mindset can serve as a catalyst, setting positive changes in your life in motion and creating a ripple effect that extends to all aspects of your being. Consider the day I decided to conquer my fear of public speaking. Initially, the thought of addressing a large audience filled me with dread. But then, I applied the warrior mindset. I saw this challenge not as a hurdle but an opportunity for growth. I prepared, practised, and visualised success; when the day came, I stepped onto the stage, my heart racing but my resolve firm.
What resulted was more than just a successful speech. This single act of courage transformed my professional life, opening up new opportunities. It boosted my confidence,

making me realise I could conquer other fears too. It expanded my network, leading to connections and friendships that enriched my life. And this is the essence of the warrior mindset - it doesn't just change one aspect of your life; it creates a positive domino effect. You're not just transforming a situation when you embrace challenges, demonstrate resilience, and take ownership of your actions. You're changing your life. In the coming chapters, we will delve into each component of the warrior mindset in more detail, from resilience and determination to adaptability and focus. We will explore actionable strategies and practical exercises that can help you harness the power of the warrior mindset to create positive changes in your life. Remember, this isn't about becoming a different person. It's about recognising and nurturing the inner strength and potential that you already possess. It's about learning to view life through a lens that empowers you to conquer challenges, grow from adversity, and transform your life.

The Journey Ahead: Unleashing Your Inner Warrior

Embarking on this journey towards adopting the warrior mindset is not about becoming a new person. Instead, it's about rekindling the primal spark within you, the inherent strength and resilience that often get lost in the hustle and bustle of our daily lives. It's about owning your life and becoming the author of your narrative. Challenges and triumphs filled my journey of cultivating the warrior mindset. The journey has been both exhilarating and demanding, from launching my own business to conquering my fear of public speaking and overcoming personal setbacks. But each challenge beat, each fear faced, has taken me one step closer to my authentic self, to a life of purpose and fulfilment. As we embark on this journey together, remember this path is sometimes linear. There will be setbacks, moments of doubt, and days when progress seems painfully slow or non-existent. But that's okay. Because adopting the warrior mindset is not about achieving perfection; it's about growth, striving to be better than we were yesterday, and embracing challenges as opportunities for learning and self-improvement. In the following chapters, we'll delve deeper into the core components of the warrior mindset, providing practical strategies and insights to help you embrace challenges, cultivate resilience, and transform your life. We'll discuss the importance of adaptability, focus, and discipline in personal growth and success. We'll explore the role of mental and emotional resilience, habits' power, relationships' importance, and the essence of living authentically. Your journey starts now. The warrior is ready and waiting. It's time to unleash your potential, conquer challenges, and transform your life. Let's take this journey together.

A Call to Action: Embrace the Warrior Within

This book, dear reader, is your call to action. It's an invitation to step into your power and transform your life from the inside out. All of us can unleash an inner warrior waiting in all of us. A part of us that is resilient, strong, adaptable, and focused. It's the part of us that is not afraid to face challenges and knows we can overcome anything that comes our way. Your inner warrior is the voice that says, "You can do this," when everything else seems to suggest otherwise. The inner strength pushes you to keep going when things get tough. It's the determination that helps you to persevere in the face of adversity and the resilience that allows you to bounce back from setbacks more robust and wiser. Embracing your inner warrior means taking responsibility for your life. It means not waiting for things to change but being the change you wish to see. It's about setting ambitious goals, pursuing them with tenacity, and never giving up, no matter your challenges. In the following chapters, we will explore the warrior mindset in detail, dissecting its core components and providing practical steps for cultivating it in your own life. From understanding the power of resilience to mastering the art of adaptability, from harnessing your focus to embracing self-discipline, we will delve into the intricacies of the warrior mindset. It's time to unleash your inner warrior, embrace your potential, and transform your life. The journey may not be easy, but I assure you, it will be worth it. After all, the most splendid victories often come from the most significant challenges.

An Ongoing Journey: The Path of the Warrior

Now that we've laid out the foundations of the warrior mindset, I want to remind you of something crucial. Adopting the warrior mindset isn't a one-time event. It's not a destination to reach. It is a continuous journey, an ongoing process of growth and transformation. Being a warrior doesn't mean you'll never face challenges, nor does it imply you're invincible. It's the very opposite. Embracing your inner warrior means you'll be willing to face and overcome those challenges head-on. It means you'll experience failure, setbacks, and adversity - but you'll use these as stepping stones to become more robust, resilient, and adaptable. Just as a warrior trains and prepares for battle, we must train our minds and hearts to withstand the trials of life. We must strive to improve, learn, adapt, and grow. It is the essence of the warrior mindset. As you move forward, there will be times when you stumble or fall. Remember, each setback is a setup for a comeback. Every failure, every mistake, is an opportunity to learn and grow. In the subsequent chapters of this book, I'll be your guide on this journey, providing you with the tools and strategies you need to foster and maintain your warrior mindset. We'll delve into how you can develop mental resilience, cultivate adaptability, build habits contributing to success, and nurture relationships that aid your personal growth. This journey will be challenging. It requires effort, commitment, and perseverance. But remember, the most rewarding paths are often the most difficult. It's time for you to rise, unleash your inner warrior, and take control of your destiny.

Are you ready?

Reflect and Act

As we conclude this chapter, take a moment to reflect on your mindset.

How do you typically react to challenges and setbacks?

Are there areas in your life where you can apply the Warrior Mindset principles?

 Grab your phone, open up your notes app, and jot down three challenges you currently face and how you could approach them with the Warrior Mindset. What steps will you take this week to start this transformation?

Remember, the journey of a warrior begins with a single step.

What will yours be?

Chapter 2

Discovering Your Inner Strength

Cultivating Mental and Emotional Resilience

Introduction to Inner Strength and Resilience

As we begin this new chapter of our journey together, I'd like to introduce you to two fundamental aspects of the warrior mindset - inner strength and resilience. Understanding these two powerful attributes is critical to cultivating our striving attitude.

So, what is inner strength? Think of it as the core of your character, the source from which your perseverance, determination, and integrity spring. That internal reservoir of power and resolve allows you to face adversity and persist when things get tough. Despite the odds stacked against you, Inner strength fuels your drive to keep going. Resilience is the extraordinary ability to adapt to change, bounce back from setbacks, and keep moving forward despite obstacles. Your psychological elasticity enables you to face challenges, manage stress, and recover from hardships or life-changing events. Resilience isn't about avoiding difficulties but learning, growing, and emerging stronger.

You might wonder why inner strength and resilience are so important. As we venture deeper into the concept of the warrior mindset, you'll understand that these traits form the backbone of this transformative mental framework. They enable us to face life's uncertainties with courage, remain calm under pressure, and bounce back from failures while keeping our sights set firmly on our goals. I want to share a story with you as an introduction to the profound power of inner strength and resilience. It's about a dear friend who has been a living embodiment of these principles.

This friend, let's call him Mark, experienced a challenging period in his life. After losing his job during a corporate restructuring, he battled feelings of worthlessness and anxiety. However, instead of succumbing to despair, Mark decided to view this setback as an opportunity for growth.

Tapping into his inner strength, he started his own business. Fueled by his resilience, Mark endured long hours, financial instability, and numerous obstacles. But he persisted, learned from his mistakes, and eventually, his business thrived. Mark's story is a testament to the transformative power of inner strength and resilience. It vividly illustrates how a warrior mindset can lead to incredible personal growth and success. But remember, Mark wasn't born with this mindset. He cultivated it. And you can too. As we journey through this chapter, I will guide you on building and harnessing your inner strength and resilience, just like Mark did.

The Power of Inner Strength

Let's start with inner strength. Like a silent, invisible force, it underpins everything we do. We're not necessarily born with it but cultivate and refine it over time through experiences and introspection. Inner strength is about our ability to control our thoughts, emotions, and actions in ways that help us navigate life's ups and downs. It helps us withstand hardships, persevere in adversity, and remain true to our values. Take a moment to reflect on your life. Can you think of a time when you were in a challenging situation, perhaps facing an insurmountable problem? Maybe you were dealing with a personal loss, a career transition, or a relationship issue. How did you handle it? If you're like most people, you might have felt overwhelmed at first, but eventually, you found a way to deal with it, to navigate the stormy seas of adversity. That's your inner strength in action. It gives you the courage to face your fears, the determination to persist in the face of obstacles, and the grit to endure, even when things seem hopeless. Inner strength is also about managing your emotions and responses to different situations. It's about staying calm amid chaos, not letting anger or frustration take over when things don't go as planned, and maintaining a positive attitude, even in the face of negativity. Remember, your inner strength is like a muscle - it gets stronger the more you use it. So how do we build this muscle? We do it by challenging ourselves, stepping outside our comfort zones, and embracing new experiences. Take out your phone again, and jot down a few challenging situations or experiences you've had recently. Note down how you responded to them and how you felt afterwards. Keep this note handy - we'll revisit it in the later sections as we discuss ways to build further and harness your inner strength. As we move forward in this chapter, we'll explore practical strategies and exercises to strengthen this vital aspect of the warrior mindset. We'll delve into how you can effectively manage your emotions, persist in adversity, and use your inner strength to fuel your journey towards personal growth and success.

Embracing Discomfort and Uncertainty

It's human nature to avoid discomfort and uncertainty. We all prefer predictability and ease, don't we? But here's the catch - growth and comfort don't coexist. To truly grow, expand our capabilities, and reach our full potential, we must be willing to embrace discomfort and uncertainty. Why is this so crucial in cultivating a warrior mindset? Because discomfort often signifies that we're on the brink of learning something new or developing a new skill. And uncertainty? It's a sign that we're venturing into uncharted territory, where real growth happens. I remember a time when I was incredibly nervous about public speaking. Standing in front of a large crowd and delivering a speech was nerve-wracking. But I knew I had to face this fear to grow or expand my horizons. So, I took on speaking engagements, practised relentlessly, and improved over time. The nerves didn't disappear entirely - they still crop up now and then - but I've learned to embrace them as part of the process. That's the power of embracing discomfort and uncertainty. Discomfort and uncertainty are not your enemies - they are catalysts for growth. They are opportunities disguised as challenges. When you start viewing them from this lens, you'll realise that they are not obstacles but stepping stones towards your personal growth.

 Open your notes app again and list a few situations where you avoided discomfort or feared uncertainty. It could be a challenging task at work, a difficult conversation with a friend, or an opportunity to try something new.

Now, consider how embracing the discomfort or uncertainty in these situations could have sparked growth. As we progress through this chapter, we'll delve deeper into strategies and techniques to better embrace pain and tension, leveraging them for your development.
Remember, discomfort and uncertainty are inevitable parts of life, but how you respond to them makes all the difference. As we navigate this section, we will uncover ways to turn these seemingly intimidating aspects into powerful instruments for personal development.

Taking Calculated Risks

Now that we've discussed embracing discomfort and uncertainty. Let's delve into another aspect of the warrior mindset — taking calculated risks. It doesn't mean recklessly throwing caution to the wind and taking unnecessary chances. No, a calculated risk is a thoughtfully assessed decision where you consider the potential drawbacks and benefits. Consider my journey into entrepreneurship. Leaving a stable job and entering the business world was a risk, but it wasn't a blind leap of faith. It was a calculated decision. I did my homework, evaluated the market, created a detailed business plan, and weighed the pros and cons. Was there a chance of failure? Absolutely. But there was also the potential for significant personal growth and success, which was worth the risk. Taking calculated risks is about assessing the situation, making an informed decision, and having the courage to take action, even when the outcome is uncertain. It's about being proactive and decisive rather than passive and reactive.

 Grab your phone and bring up your notes app again. Think about a time when you took a calculated risk. Write it down. What was the situation? What was the risk involved? How did you assess the pros and cons?
And most importantly, what was the outcome?

It's okay if the risk didn't lead to the desired result. The important part is that you took a step, learned something valuable, and grew from the experience. Taking calculated risks pushes your boundaries and opens up new possibilities. It can be scary, but remember, having a warrior mindset is about courage in fear. And as we'll see in the upcoming sections, it's also about learning from your experiences and using them as stepping stones towards personal growth.

Learning from Mistakes

What separates warriors from others is their attitude towards failure. Those with a warrior mindset do not view failure as a final destination but as a learning opportunity. They understand that mistakes and failures are a part of life and a vital part of the journey towards personal growth and success. Let's take a moment to reflect on my early days as an entrepreneur. There were numerous occasions when things didn't go as planned. Launches that flopped, marketing strategies that failed, and countless other setbacks that could have discouraged me. But did I throw in the towel? No. I chose to view each of these 'failures' as an opportunity to learn and grow.

I took the time to understand what went wrong, adjusted my strategies, and tried again. It is the power of learning from your mistakes. It shifts your perspective from seeing failure as something to avoid to view it as an invaluable teacher.

 Pick up your phone and open your notes app. Write down a situation where you experienced failure or made a significant mistake. How did it make you feel? What did you learn from the experience? How did it help you grow or change your approach?

We all make mistakes, We all experience failure. But with a warrior mindset, you'll see these not as dead ends but as stepping stones towards your ultimate goal. This attitude, this resilience in the face of adversity, fuels personal growth and paves the way for success. And as we'll discuss in the following sections, this resilience and learning-oriented approach enable you to bounce back more vital than ever.

Bouncing Back Stronger

Possessing a warrior mindset means bouncing back stronger after a setback. Resilience is not just about surviving adversity, but learning and growing from it, emerging more robust and capable than before. Think back to the career transition I spoke about earlier, shifting from the predictability and security of a corporate job to the uncertain world of entrepreneurship. Many times, I faced significant obstacles that tested my resolve. But each challenge only made me more resilient. Every setback and failure was an opportunity to learn and come back stronger. Let's look at this through the lens of physical training. When you lift weights, you cause damage to your muscle fibres. But this damage triggers the body's repair process, causing the muscles to grow back stronger. It is the essence of resilience

— growing more robust through adversity. It's now time to pick up your phone again.

 In your notes app, write about a time when you faced a significant setback. How did you respond? How did it change you? What lessons did you learn, and how did it contribute to your growth?

If you have yet to face such a setback, think about how to apply the warrior mindset when you inevitably do. Remember, the warrior mindset is not about never failing or avoiding adversity. It's about using these experiences to fuel growth and as stepping stones towards your goals. Resilience, my friend, is a defining trait of the warrior mindset. And as you'll see in the next section, it's not the only one.

Embracing Continuous Learning

The final aspect of the warrior mindset we'll discuss in this chapter is continuous learning. Warriors are lifelong learners, constantly seeking to improve their skills, broaden their knowledge, and deepen their understanding.
In my journey, continuous learning has been instrumental. Whether it was learning the ropes of entrepreneurship, honing my public speaking skills, or understanding the science behind habit formation, I was always in a state of learning. And this constant pursuit of knowledge helped me to grow and achieve my goals.
Take, for example, my struggle with public speaking. When I first decided to overcome this fear, I didn't just throw myself onto the stage without preparation. I took the time to learn. I researched effective communication techniques, studied great speakers, and practised diligently. My commitment to

learning enabled me to conquer my fear and become a confident public speaker.

Now, think about the areas where you can embrace continuous learning.

 Grab your phone and open your notes app again. Jot down a few skills or subjects you'd like to learn more about. They could be related to your career, personal interests, or even a new hobby you want to try.

But remember, learning isn't just about gathering information. It's about applying and integrating what you learn into your daily life. The warrior doesn't only learn for the sake of learning but to enrich their lives, solve problems, and reach their goals.

As we close this chapter, remember that the warrior mindset is not a destination but a journey. It's about developing resilience, adopting a growth mindset, facing fears, stepping out of your comfort zone, setting ambitious goals, and embracing continuous learning. In the following chapters, we'll delve deeper into these aspects and explore practical strategies for cultivating your warrior mindset.

So, are you ready to take the next step on this journey? I hope so because the journey of a warrior is about to get even more exciting. Onward, brave warrior!

Action Points
1. Reflect on Your Current Mindset: What beliefs and attitudes serve you well? What limiting beliefs are holding you back? Write these down in your notes app.
2. Identify Areas for Growth: Choose one area where you can apply the warrior mindset. It could be a personal goal, a professional aspiration, or a relationship challenge. Write it down and keep it in focus.
3. Set a Learning Goal: Choose a new skill or topic you'd like to learn more about. It can be anything that aligns with your personal or professional growth. Note this in your app and start researching resources to help you learn.

Remember, the journey of a thousand miles begins with a single step. So, start small, be consistent, and celebrate your progress. You're on your way to cultivating a warrior mindset and unlocking your full potential!

Chapter 3

The Building Blocks of the Warrior Mindset

Introduction

Hello again, warriors in training! As we move forward in our journey, we're about to delve deeper into the essence of the warrior mindset. Having established the foundations and explored some preliminary strategies, we're now ready to identify and understand the core building blocks of the warrior mindset. Build your warrior mindset, and form the pillars of strength upon these critical traits. In this chapter, we will dissect each attribute, one by one, revealing its importance and role in fostering resilience, personal growth, and unshakeable strength. We will dive into my personal experiences and lessons learned, along with actionable tips and techniques to cultivate these essential traits within yourself. We'll be discussing seven key attributes: courage, resilience, discipline, adaptability, perseverance, empathy, and the practice of self-reflection coupled with a growth mindset. Some of these traits may already be familiar, while others might be new concepts. Either way, we will delve into each one in detail, unpacking their significance, exploring their application, and looking at how we can develop and strengthen these traits within ourselves. But remember, this isn't a checklist. These aren't boxes to be ticked off once and forgotten. Instead, consider these traits as muscles. As we work out to build and strengthen our physical muscles, we must also exercise these mental and emotional "muscles" to develop our warrior mindset. This process is ongoing, evolving with each new experience and challenge. So, are you ready to discover the building blocks of the warrior mindset? Let's dive right in, starting with our first attribute: courage.

Courage

When we talk about warriors, the trait that often comes to mind first is courage. Courage is an essential pillar of the warrior mindset, forming the backbone of our actions and decisions. It isn't the absence of fear, as some may think, but the ability to take action despite our fears. If you recall the story I shared in Chapter 1 about confronting my fear of public speaking, you'll remember that I felt fear but didn't let it hold me back. I want you to understand that it's natural to feel afraid when stepping out of your comfort zone. Courage isn't about being fearless; it's about acknowledging your fears, confronting them, and pushing forward anyway. It's about deciding that the potential reward on the other side of fear is worth the risk. Each of us has our own set of fears or worries. For some, it might be the fear of failure or rejection. For others, it might be the fear of change or uncertainty. Regardless of what your fears are, embracing courage means choosing to face these fears head-on.
Here's an exercise for you.

Open your notes app on your phone and jot down some fears holding you back from pursuing your goals or living authentically. Write them down and acknowledge their presence.

In the following sections, we'll explore strategies to face and overcome these fears, transforming them from barriers into stepping stones. Just remember, courage is like a muscle. The more you use it, the stronger it gets. With each act of courage, small or large, you're building your warrior mindset, bit by bit.

Resilience

Resilience, the capacity to recover quickly from difficulties, is another vital component of the warrior mindset. Life has a way of throwing curveballs at us. Unexpected challenges and setbacks can knock us down. Still, our ability to bounce back, adapt, and grow from these experiences defines our warrior spirit. I want to remind you of the personal setback I faced, which I shared with you in Chapter 1. It was a challenging time, filled with emotion and confusion. But it was also a pivotal moment that sparked my newfound resilience. I want you to remember that it's through adversity that we often uncover our most vital selves. We discover abilities and strengths that we didn't know we had. Let's consider an exercise to reinforce this concept.

 In your notes app, write down a recent or past challenge that knocked you off your feet. How did it affect you? What lessons did you learn from it? How did you grow from that experience?

This reflection can help you understand how resilience has played a role in your life and how it can help you move forward. Remember, warriors don't view setbacks as permanent failures but temporary obstacles. They see adversity as an opportunity for growth and learning. Embrace this mindset, and you'll be well on your way to building the resilience of a warrior.

Discipline

The warrior mindset is complete with discipline. You might have grand visions and excellent strategies. Still, achieving your goals will be incredibly challenging without discipline. Discipline keeps us on track, pushes us to take action, and helps us follow through with our commitments, even when it's uncomfortable or difficult.

Remember my experience with fitness that I shared in Chapter 1? Discipline pushed me to wake up early each morning and maintain a strict diet. Despite the initial discomfort, I stuck with it because I knew it was essential for achieving my goals. That's what discipline is all about committing to your objectives and consistently working towards them, regardless of how you're feeling. Let's put this into practice.

 On your notes app, write down one goal you want to achieve. List the consistent actions you need to take to achieve this goal. How can you incorporate these actions into your daily routine? How will you stay committed when feeling unmotivated or faced with distractions?

Remember, achieving greatness isn't about doing extraordinary things but about doing ordinary things extraordinarily well, consistently. It's the power of discipline, a critical part of the warrior mindset.

Self-reflection and Self-assessment

Having a warrior mindset doesn't mean charging mindlessly into battle. It's about understanding yourself, your strengths, weaknesses, and values to align your actions with your goals and aspirations. When I faced significant setbacks in my personal life, self-reflection was a vital part of my recovery. It allowed me to pause and gain a deeper understanding of myself. I assessed my reactions, explored my feelings, and evaluated my choices. This process of introspection gave me a clearer perspective and helped me navigate the challenges with more resilience and wisdom.

Let's translate this into an exercise you can use right now. Open your notes app and jot down your answers to these questions:
1. What are my core values?
2. What are my strengths? How can I leverage them more effectively?
3. What are my weaknesses? How can they hinder me, and what can I do to overcome or mitigate them?

4. How do my values align with my current goals and actions?
5. What changes can I make to better align my actions with my values and goals?

Take your time with this exercise. Take the time to explore your thoughts and feelings. This self-reflection and self-assessment exercise is not a one-time thing; make it a regular practice. It will provide valuable insights and keep you grounded in your journey towards adopting the warrior mindset.

The Role of Mentorship

A rarely discussed aspect of the warrior mindset is the role of mentorship. It might seem counterintuitive. After all, isn't the warrior often portrayed as a lone wolf, standing against the odds by himself? But that's a myth. The true warrior knows the value of learning from others. In my journey, I've been fortunate to have mentors who have guided, challenged, and helped me grow. Their wisdom and experiences have saved me from numerous pitfalls and accelerated my growth. You, too, can benefit immensely from having a mentor who's walked the path before you. They won't do the work for you, but they can provide valuable insights, feedback, and guidance to smooth your journey. Let's put this into practice.

Open your notes app and reflect on these points:
1. Who are the people in your life that you look up to? They can be individuals from your personal and professional life or even authors and public figures whose work resonates with you.
2. What are the qualities or achievements that you admire in them?

3. How can you learn from them? Could you approach them for mentorship, or are there books, podcasts, or courses they've created that you can learn from?

Remember, mentorship isn't a one-way street. It's a collaborative relationship that requires effort and engagement from both sides. So be proactive, ask thoughtful questions, and show your commitment to learning and growth. This practice is a valuable step in developing a warrior mindset.

Celebrating Progress

Let's talk about the importance of celebrating progress. Yes, you heard it right! Celebrating progress, no matter how small it seems, is a critical part of cultivating the warrior mindset. You see, warriors aren't just relentless fighters. They are also grateful observers of their journey. They understand the power of positive reinforcement and know that every step forward is a victory. Progress in adopting a warrior mindset is only sometimes a linear process. There will be setbacks and days when you've taken two steps back. It's easy to get discouraged in these moments, but remember, each challenge is a learning experience that brings you closer to your goal. Let's take a moment here.

Grab your phone and open up your notes app. Reflect on your journey so far. What progress have you made? What lessons have you learned? Have you become more resilient, disciplined, or self-aware? Write down all your achievements, big and small, and take a moment to celebrate them.

Developing a warrior mindset is not about perfection but growth. It's about becoming a better version of yourself with each passing day. So take pride in your progress, reward your efforts, and use your achievements as fuel to propel you further on your journey. It's your journey; every step you take towards growth is a victory worth celebrating.

Embracing Continuous Learning

If there is one thing that warriors value, it's the pursuit of knowledge. They understand that growth is born out of learning and that to stand still is to stagnate. The more we know, the more we grow and the more capable we become. The concept of Kaizen, a Japanese philosophy meaning "continuous improvement," is integral to the warrior mindset. Warriors understand that their growth doesn't end when they've reached their goals; it is a never-ending personal development journey.
Remember when we talked about the importance of maintaining an open mind? Here's where it truly shines. By keeping our minds open, we allow ourselves to absorb new knowledge, seek learning opportunities, and constantly push the boundaries of our abilities.

 So, take out your notes app once again and reflect. What new skills or knowledge can support your journey? It could be a book on self-discipline, a course on emotional intelligence, or a podcast on resilience. Write down three new things you want to learn this month that align with your goals.

Never stop learning, my friend. A warrior knows that each new piece of knowledge and skill brings them closer to their true potential. Embrace this continuous learning journey, and you'll be amazed at how far you can go.

The Power of Mentorship

Every warrior has a guide and a mentor who helps illuminate their path. The role of a mentor is invaluable in our journey towards adopting the warrior mindset. They've been there, faced the struggles, and emerged victorious. Their experience, wisdom, and guidance can save us from countless pitfalls and help us navigate our path more confidently and clearly. My mentors have significantly shaped my journey. They've not only shared their knowledge and experiences and challenged me, pushing me to question my assumptions, step out of my comfort zone, and strive for excellence. Their faith in my potential, even when I doubted myself was a powerful motivator that spurred me on. Now, it's your turn to identify potential mentors who can guide your journey. These could be people you admire, individuals whose journeys resonate with your own, or experts with a wealth of knowledge in areas you wish to grow. Remember, a mentor does not necessarily need to be someone you have direct access to. They could also be authors of books, speakers in TED Talks, or thought leaders sharing valuable content online.

 Open up your notes app once more, and write down the names of three potential mentors. Beside each name, note what you admire about them and what you hope to learn. Then, make it your goal to reach out to them or engage with their content.

Having a mentor does not mean giving up your autonomy or mindlessly following someone else's path. Instead, it means being humble enough to acknowledge that we can learn from others' experiences and wise enough to adapt their teachings to our unique journey.

Conclusion - Applying the Warrior Mindset

We've journeyed far into the heart of the warrior mindset in this chapter. Together, we have explored the key elements of the philosophy: resilience, self-awareness, discipline, authenticity, courage, and mentorship. Each one is a vital component of the warrior mindset, and they all intertwine, creating a robust framework for personal growth and transformation.

Now, the challenge lies in applying these principles in your life. Remember, the warrior mindset isn't about perfection. It's about perseverance, picking yourself up after a setback, dusting yourself off, and trying again with more knowledge and understanding.

First, I encourage you to review your notes from this chapter. Reflect on the areas we've discussed and identify which resonates most with you. Where can you see the potential for immediate change? Which areas will require longer-term commitment and discipline? What resources and support do you need to help you in this journey?

Finally, remember the power of mentorship. Be bold and seek guidance and learn from those who've walked the path before you. Embrace the wisdom of others, but always remember to adapt it to your unique journey and circumstances.

As we close this chapter, I hope you feel inspired, empowered, and ready to start your journey towards the warrior mindset. Let's continue to the next chapter, where we will explore specific strategies and techniques that can help you cultivate and maintain your warrior mindset.

Chapter 4

Strategies to Cultivate the Warrior Mindset

Introduction

Our journey together isn't just about understanding the warrior mindset; it's about making it a part of who you are and your identity. So, we've reached the heart of the matter: how to cultivate this mindset within yourself.

This chapter is akin to a map, charting out the route you can follow, replete with the strategies and exercises that will act as your compass. It's the practical element of our exploration, where you apply all the concepts discussed in the previous chapters to your everyday life.

We will delve into various techniques, from visualisation to mindfulness, consider the role of physical conditioning, explore the power of a growth mindset, and look at the value of a personal mantra. We'll also discuss the importance of a strong support network, setting realistic yet challenging goals, and establishing consistent rituals.

Each of these components is like a brick, a fundamental building block. Individually, they may seem simple, but together they form the formidable fortress of the warrior mindset.

Remember, transformation isn't a spectator sport. It requires active participation and consistent practice. As you review this chapter, please read and truly engage with the content. Try the exercises, reflect on the insights, and start making notes of the strategies that resonate with you in your phone notes app.

This journey may not always be easy, but trust me when I say it will be worth it. Because the power and potential you can unlock with the warrior mindset are limitless.

Are you ready? Let's begin.

Embrace the Power of Visualisation

Do you remember how we would let our imaginations run wild when we were children? We could be astronauts on a mission to Mars, firefighters saving the day, or explorers on a grand adventure. As children, the power of our imagination was limitless. This power and visualisation ability is potent in cultivating the warrior mindset. The concept of visualisation isn't new. Professional athletes, high-performing executives, and successful individuals use it widely. And no, it's not just daydreaming. Visualisation is mentally rehearsing or imagining a specific event, outcome, or scenario. It involves seeing, feeling, and experiencing it before it happens.

When you visualise your success, you set the stage for your mind and body to follow through. Our brains are fascinating, and they often have trouble distinguishing between what is real and vividly imagined. When you imagine something with detail and emotion, your brain starts believing it's real. This process primes your brain to act in a way that is consistent with what you have imagined.

Now, how do you apply this? You can start by visualising your goals. Picture yourself achieving these goals as vividly as possible, down to the minutest detail. Feel the emotions, hear the sounds, and immerse yourself in that moment of success. Repeat this visualisation regularly, and you'll find that your belief in your ability to achieve your goals will strengthen.

Here's an exercise for you: Open up your notes app, write down one of your goals, and then detail the scene of you achieving that goal. Engage all your senses in this imagination exercise. Then, find a quiet spot, close your eyes, and play this scene repeatedly in your mind.

Do this daily and observe how it affects your mindset and progress towards your goal.

Remember, the warrior knows the destination before starting the journey. Visualisation is your way of defining that destination and seeing the victory before the battle has even begun.

Developing Resilience Through Adversity

As we journey towards a warrior mindset, it's essential to remember that even the most prepared warriors face challenges. Life is unpredictable, and it's often through adversity that we grow the most. Unpredictability is where resilience comes into play.

Resilience is our ability to bounce back from hardships, keep moving forward despite obstacles, and remain steadfast in adversity. Resilience is an integral part of the warrior mindset. When life pushes a warrior down, they don't stay down. They get back up, dust themselves off, and keep fighting.

I was initially overwhelmed when I faced a significant setback in my personal life. I struggled and doubted myself, but then, I recalled the warrior mindset and realised it was an opportunity to grow. By focusing on resilience, I found the strength to keep moving forward, to persist through the challenge. Today, the experience was instrumental in shaping the person I am now.

Now, you might wonder, "How can I develop resilience?" One of the most effective ways is through exposing yourself to controlled adversity. Intentionally placing yourself in situations that push your boundaries, stretch your comfort zone, or challenge you. It's like exercising a muscle; the more you work it out, the stronger it gets. It could be anything from taking on a challenging project at work to pushing yourself physically through intense workouts or even complex deep-seated fears.

Here's a task for you. In your notes app, write down one situation or activity you've been avoiding because it scares or challenges you. Next to it, write down one step you can take towards facing this challenge.

Remember, it's not about eliminating fear or discomfort. It's about proving that you can face, survive, and grow from it. Don't shy away from adversity. Embrace, learn from, and use it to build your resilience. It is the path of the warrior, a path of growth, transformation, and, ultimately, mastery.

The Power of Discipline and Consistency

Achieving greatness in any aspect of life requires two essential elements: discipline and consistency. The warrior mindset recognises the transformative power of these two elements and integrates them into daily life. When I set out to achieve my fitness goals, I quickly realised that more than sporadic effort would be necessary. I needed discipline - a commitment to adhering to my fitness plan regardless of how I felt on any particular day. I needed consistency - the commitment to show up, day after day, even when progress seemed slow. One key thing I learned during this process was that discipline and consistency were not about perfection. There were days I faltered, days when I gave in to temptation, and days when I didn't hit my targets. But instead of allowing these moments to derail my journey, I learned to view them as part of the process. Discipline is not about never falling but always getting back up. Consistency is not about never missing a day but never quitting.

So here's a task for you. Grab your phone and open up that notes app. Write down one area where you'd like to cultivate more discipline and consistency. Next to it, write down your daily actions to make it a reality.

It could be a health goal, a career goal, or even a personal development goal. No matter what it is, remember, the key is to show up for yourself, day after day, no matter how small the action may seem.

Discipline and consistency are the undercurrents that drive the warrior mindset, leading to transformation and growth. Embrace these powerful elements and watch as they change your life.

Turning Setbacks into Comebacks

Let's talk about setbacks. They are inevitable, no matter who you are or what you're trying to achieve. You may face obstacles that threaten to derail your plans. However, the warrior mindset helps turn setbacks into comebacks.

I remember a time when I faced a significant personal setback. I felt overwhelmed, unsure of how to navigate the situation. But, by leveraging the warrior mindset, I didn't allow the setback to define me. Instead, I used it to drive my resilience and foster my growth.

So, what does this look like in practical terms? It's about shifting perspective. Instead of seeing a setback as an insurmountable obstacle, consider it an opportunity to learn, adapt, and grow stronger. It's about perseverance, tenacity, and the determination to keep moving forward, regardless of the circumstances.

Now, grab your phone, open your notes app, and jot down an instance where a setback took a toll on you. Write down what you learned from it and how you could use that experience to cultivate resilience.

This process will not only help you reflect on your journey and provide a roadmap for navigating future challenges. The warrior mindset understands that setbacks are not roadblocks; they're detours, often leading us towards unexpected paths of growth and learning. Remember, every setback is a setup for an even more significant comeback.

Building Discipline and Consistency

In embracing the warrior mindset, discipline and consistency play pivotal roles. These key ingredients are necessary for even the most ambitious dreams and strategies to succeed. I remember setting some big fitness goals for myself. They required me to wake up early for workouts, maintain a strict diet, and consistently push myself out of my comfort zone. Initially, it seemed challenging, but I knew that with the warrior mindset, I could harness the power of discipline and consistency.

Cultivating discipline is crucial to create a routine. Set clear objectives and align your daily activities to these goals. Consistency, on the other hand, is all about repetition. It's about doing what needs to be done, even when you don't feel like doing it. Over time, these consistent actions become ingrained habits, leading to lasting changes.

Now, it's your turn.

Grab your phone and open your notes app. Write down one goal that requires discipline and consistency from you. List the steps you need to take daily or weekly to achieve this goal.

Keep track of your progress, and celebrate your small victories. It's these little steps that culminate in significant changes.

Cultivating discipline and consistency is like honing your inner warrior. These traits form the backbone of the warrior mindset, enabling you to conquer any challenge that comes your way.

Strengthening Your Mental Resilience

Now we're heading towards an aspect of the warrior mindset that has been my rock during challenging times: mental resilience. Building mental strength is like forging a sword; it requires patience, dedication, and repeated exposure to the flames of adversity.

I remember a time when I faced a significant personal setback. It felt like a sudden storm had hit me, and I was lost at sea, struggling to keep afloat. During this time, I learned the importance of resilience in the warrior mindset.

Mental resilience is about maintaining a positive outlook and not allowing setbacks to break your spirit. It's about viewing challenges as opportunities for growth rather than obstacles. It's about finding the strength to stand up when knocked down.

Open your notes app again. Reflect on a time when you faced a significant challenge. How did you react? What did you learn? How has that experience shaped you? Write it down.

This reflection is the foundation upon which we'll build your mental resilience. Building mental strength is a vital part of the warrior mindset, providing you with the grit and determination to face any storm that comes your way.

Cultivating Patience and Persistence

As we progress on this journey, I want to highlight two pillars that hold up the warrior mindset - patience and persistence. There's a saying I often remind myself of when things get tough, "The bamboo that bends is stronger than the oak that resists." This quote encapsulates the essence of patience and persistence. Like a bamboo tree, a true warrior must be patient enough to weather the storm and persistent enough to keep pushing forward no matter what. For instance, I only saw results after I started my entrepreneurial journey. It took months, even years, of hard work, perseverance, and many failures. Sometimes I felt like giving up, but I reminded myself of the warrior mindset of patience and persistence.

Open your notes app once more. I want you to think about a goal you've had that seemed impossible at first. Did you persist? Did you show patience? If you had given up, what could you have done differently? If you succeeded, how did patience and persistence play a role? Jot these reflections down.

Patience and perseverance are like two sides of the same coin. They complement each other, fostering a resilient and determined mindset, a true warrior's mindset.

Embracing Change

Another cornerstone of the warrior mindset is the ability to adapt to change. We often fear change because it brings uncertainty and challenges our comfort zones. But think about it, has a warrior ever won battles without adapting to changing circumstances? Let me share my experience with you. The corporate world was familiar territory for me.

However, everything was new and unknown when I embarked on my entrepreneurial journey. There were countless times when things didn't go as planned, and I had to change my strategies, adapt to new market trends, and even deal with sudden roadblocks. If I had resisted these changes, I wouldn't be where I am today.

I want you to pick up your notes app and think about a time when you had to adapt to a significant change in your life. How did you handle it? What were the results? How did this experience shape you as an individual? Write these down.

Remember, as water flows around obstacles and finds its path, a true warrior learns to adapt to changes and turns them into opportunities. The warrior mindset is not rigid; it's flexible, adaptable, and open to new experiences.

The Power of Persistence

Let's discuss another critical facet of the warrior mindset - persistence. Many times in life, we set out to accomplish something. Still, it's tempting to retreat when we encounter resistance or difficulty. However, through persistence, warriors, and indeed any successful individuals, achieve their goals.

During my entrepreneurial journey, there were numerous obstacles, and many times, things went differently than planned. It would have been easier to give up, to return to the comfort and stability of my old job. But I persisted. I believed in my vision, my purpose, and most importantly, I believed in myself.

I want you to pull up your notes app again. Reflect on your own experiences where you've shown persistence. It could be a project at work, a personal fitness goal, or a challenging course you took. Note how you felt during the process and the outcome achieved due to your persistence.

This reflection can be a source of inspiration for you when you meet obstacles in the future. In the grand scheme of things, challenges and setbacks are temporary. Remember, warriors, do not give up; they persist until they achieve their goals. The journey of a thousand miles begins with a single step but continues with each subsequent stage. Your journey towards cultivating a warrior mindset requires persistence.

Recap and Action Plan

As we wrap up this chapter on the warrior mindset's intrinsic components, I want to take a moment to recap and reinforce the key points we've explored:

- We've delved into the importance of setting and working towards goals, understanding that warriors are always clear about their mission.
- We discussed the power of self-belief and how warriors trust their abilities and skills to overcome challenges.
- We emphasised the significance of resilience, understanding that warriors aren't immune to setbacks but have the mental strength to bounce back.
- We also discussed discipline and consistency, recognising that warriors are dedicated to their purpose and consistently taking action.
- And finally, we underscored the importance of persistence, realising that warriors don't give up in the face of adversity; they persist until they achieve their goals.

As an action plan, please identify one area from each component you'd like to work on. Write down specific actions you plan to take to enhance these aspects of your warrior mindset.

Review your reflections and notes regularly and adjust your action plan as needed. Becoming a warrior is a journey of continuous growth and evolution. The warrior mindset isn't just about overcoming challenges; it's about becoming a better version of ourselves.

Chapter 5
Developing Mental Resilience

Understanding Mental Resilience

In the previous chapters, we discussed the fundamentals of the warrior mindset, how to build mental toughness, and practical strategies to overcome adversity. Now, let's delve into an equally important concept: Mental Resilience. Simply put, mental resilience is the capacity to recover quickly from difficulties, bounce back from adversity and keep moving forward. The inner strength allows you to handle stress, overcome obstacles, adapt to change, and cope with life's challenges in a healthy, constructive way. It's about mental flexibility, emotional intelligence, and perseverance. Why is mental resilience so crucial for adopting a warrior mindset? The answer lies in the nature of life itself. Life is full of ups and downs, triumphs and trials, joys and sorrows. No one is immune to challenges and setbacks. However, how you react to these challenges, how quickly you recover from them, and whether you learn and grow from these experiences all depend on your mental resilience. Just as a warrior stands firm in the face of adversity and fights tirelessly until the end, a person with mental resilience doesn't give in to challenges or setbacks. Instead, they stand up, dust themselves off, learn from the experience, and move forward stronger and wiser. In the subsequent sections of this chapter, we'll delve deeper into the components of mental resilience, why it's vital for the warrior mindset, and how you can cultivate it.

Remember, as you jot down your thoughts, reflections, and key takeaways in your notes app as you read through.

Components of Mental Resilience

As we dive deeper into mental resilience, it's vital to break it down into its key components. Understanding these components will allow us to build a holistic picture of mental strength and how it functions.

1. **Self-awareness:** The first component of mental resilience is self-awareness, the ability to recognise and understand your emotions, thoughts, and behaviours. It's about knowing your strengths and weaknesses, understanding your triggers and how you react to stress or adversity. When you are self-aware, you can manage your reactions, make conscious decisions, and adapt your behaviour as needed.
2. **Emotional Regulation:** Emotional regulation refers to your ability to manage and control your emotions, especially under stress or during challenging situations. It doesn't mean suppressing your feelings but acknowledging them, understanding their source, and expressing them in a healthy, constructive manner.
3. **Optimism:** Maintaining a positive outlook, even when facing difficulties, is crucial to mental resilience. Optimists view setbacks as temporary, isolated incidents rather than permanent, pervasive problems. They see challenges as opportunities for learning and growth, which enables them to remain hopeful and keep pushing forward.
4. **Adaptability:** Life is ever-changing and full of surprises. Hence, adapting to new circumstances, environments, or challenges is crucial to mental resilience. It's about being flexible and open-minded, learning from experiences, and adjusting your strategies.
5. **Problem-solving:** Resilient individuals see problems not as insurmountable obstacles but as puzzles to be solved. They are solution-oriented, using their creativity,

critical thinking, and resourcefulness to overcome hurdles and move closer to their goals.
6. **Persistence:** Last but not least, perseverance is critical to mental resilience. It's about staying committed to your goals and dreams, persisting through difficulties and setbacks, and refusing to give up, no matter how tough things get.

As you digest each of these components, take a moment to reflect on your level of resilience.

Use your notes app to jot down insights, thoughts, or reflections. How do you see these components playing out in your own life? In what areas do you feel strong, and where might you need to focus your development efforts?

Remember, developing mental resilience is a journey, not a destination. Be patient with yourself as we explore these components more deeply in the coming sections.

The Power of Self-Awareness

Self-awareness is an essential part of the Warrior Mindset. This crucial tool paves the way for personal growth and self-improvement. The mirror helps you look inward and understand your strengths, weaknesses, emotions, beliefs, and motivations. But what does it mean to be self-aware? It's more than knowing your likes and dislikes, ambitions and fears. Self-awareness involves understanding who you are, why you react to situations in specific ways, and how your emotions and thoughts influence your actions. With a strong self-awareness, you become conscious of the impact of your decisions, behaviour, and mindset. This awareness lets you take control, make deliberate choices, and steer your life in the desired direction. Imagine self-awareness as a navigation system for your life. Without it, you're like a ship adrift at sea, guided by the winds of external influences and circumstances. But with self-awareness, you're the ship's captain, able to navigate towards your chosen destination, regardless of the wind's direction or the sea's roughness.

Think about a situation that made you react strongly – frustration at a work project, anger towards a friend, or excitement about a new opportunity. Now, with your notes app at the ready, answer these questions:

1. What were the specific triggers for your reaction?
2. What thoughts and emotions did you experience?
3. How did these thoughts and feelings influence your actions?

The more you practice this type of self-reflection, the greater your self-awareness will become, allowing you to harness the full power of the Warrior Mindset. Remember, self-awareness isn't about being hard on yourself or criticising your actions. It's about understanding yourself better to grow, learn, and transform into the best version of yourself – surviving and thriving. Stay tuned for the next section, where we delve into the transformative power of habit formation. In the meantime, make a habit of reflecting on your actions and reactions. Your journey towards the Warrior Mindset is well underway.

The Transformative Power of Habit Formation

Habits are powerful. They can make us or break us, lift us or drag us down. But the most crucial thing about habits? We can choose them and, through them, shape our destiny. The power of habit formation lies in its ability to create sustainable change. It's not about quick fixes or temporary solutions but long-term transformation. The proper habits, repeated consistently, can significantly alter the course of our lives. Think about it - isn't it easier to stick to a routine when you do it daily without thinking rather than a massive effort you must consciously undertake? That's the power of habit. They take the struggle out of making the right choices because they become automatic. In our journey towards embracing the Warrior Mindset, cultivating positive habits is non-negotiable. Whether it's a morning meditation routine, regular physical exercise, or dedicating time for self-reflection, these routines anchor us, providing structure and stability amidst life's uncertainties. So how do we create new habits? Here are three simple yet effective steps:

1. **Start Small:** Big changes start with small steps. If you want to cultivate a habit of meditating, start with just 5 minutes a day. It's not about how much you do but rather about the consistency of doing it.
2. **Stack Habits:** Pairing a new habit with an existing one is known as habit stacking. For instance, if you want to practice gratitude, you can do it while having your morning coffee. Doing this leverages the power of established routines to help anchor your new habit.
3. **Celebrate Wins:** It's essential to acknowledge and celebrate your progress, no matter how small. These little victories create positive emotions, reinforcing the behaviour and making it more likely to stick.

Open your notes app and jot down one new habit you'd like to incorporate. Then, identify a small step you can take towards that habit, an existing habit you can stack it with, and how you'll celebrate your wins.

Habit formation is a marathon, not a sprint. It takes time, patience, and perseverance. But remember, as you're cultivating these new routines, you're not just forming habits; but transforming your life.

Stay tuned for the next section to delve into how mindset shifts can bring about radical transformation. But until then, remember: The power to change your life lies in your chosen habits.

Embracing Mindset Shifts for Radical Transformation

Once we've established empowering habits and routines, we must focus on another critical aspect of the warrior journey - shifting our mindset. Mindset, in simple terms, is a set of beliefs or attitudes we hold about ourselves and the world. Our mindset influences our behaviour, decisions, and actions, making it a potent tool for transformation. The warrior mindset isn't just about being strong and resilient. It's about acknowledging our vulnerabilities, learning from our failures, and continually seeking growth. It's about looking at challenges as opportunities and setbacks as lessons.

So how can we shift our mindset towards that of a warrior? Here are three strategies:

1. **Reframe Negative Thoughts:** Our thoughts influence our feelings, which drive our actions. By learning to reframe negative thoughts into positive ones, we can change our perspective and, consequently, our behaviour. For instance, instead of thinking, "I can't do this," try thinking, "I haven't mastered this yet, but I'm working on it."
2. **Embrace a Growth Mindset:** A growth mindset coined by psychologist Carol Dweck is the belief that you can develop abilities and intelligence through dedication and

hard work. It's about valuing the process over the result, embracing challenges, and seeing effort as a path to mastery.
3. **Practice Mindfulness:** Mindfulness is about being fully present in the moment and aware of our thoughts, feelings, and actions without judgment. It's a powerful tool that can help us stay grounded, reduce stress, and cultivate inner peace, all crucial elements of the warrior mindset.

As you venture into this journey, remember that mindset shifts don't happen overnight. They require consistent effort, patience, and practice. But the rewards are well worth the effort.

Again, take a moment to jot down in your notes app any negative thoughts you're currently wrestling with, how you might reframe them, and steps to embrace a growth mindset and practice mindfulness.

The following section discusses how to set meaningful goals and work towards them with the warrior mindset. But until then, remember: Your mindset is the lens through which you view the world. Change your mindset, and you change your world.

Setting and Pursuing Meaningful Goals

Every warrior has a mission, a purpose that drives them. For us, our goals embody that purpose. Our goals give us a direction, a tangible destination to strive towards. And with the warrior mindset, we can pursue these goals with tenacity, resilience, and determination. Here are three essential steps to set and pursue meaningful goals:

1. **Identify Your Goals:** Start by identifying what you want to achieve. It could be a career goal, a personal development goal, or a health and wellness goal. Make sure it aligns with your values, passions, and long-term vision.
2. **Make Them SMART**: Once you've identified your goals, make them SMART - Specific, Measurable, Achievable, Relevant, and Time-bound. This framework adds clarity and structure to your goals, making them more manageable and attainable.
3. **Develop a Plan of Action:** What steps will you take to achieve your goals? What resources do you need? Who can support you?

Warriors don't just set goals. They commit to them. They are disciplined and consistent in their actions. They face obstacles head-on, adapt to changes, and persist.

Now, go ahead and pull out your notes app. Write down one meaningful goal you want to achieve and use the SMART framework to define it. Then, outline a basic action plan.

As you continue your journey, remember that setting and pursuing goals is not a one-time event. It's an ongoing process that requires reflection, adaptation, and persistence. In the next section, we'll explore how to sustain your warrior mindset in the face of challenges and setbacks. Until then, keep your eyes on your goals, warrior, and remember: The journey is as important as the destination.

Resilience and Adaptability – The Warrior's Shield

As warriors, we face many challenges and adversities. They come in all shapes and sizes, testing our resolve and pushing our limits. However, equipped with our warrior mindset, we have a powerful shield against these trials: Resilience and Adaptability. Resilience is the ability to bounce back from setbacks and difficulties. It's about enduring hardships and emerging more robust on the other side. The more resilient we are, the better we can handle life's challenges and maintain our momentum towards our goals.

On the other hand, adaptability is about adjusting to new circumstances and environments. It's about learning from our experiences, being open to change, and finding innovative solutions to problems. It enables us to navigate the ever-changing landscapes of our lives and make progress, no matter what comes our way. Now, building resilience and adaptability is something that takes time to happen. It requires consistent effort and a willingness to step out of your comfort zone. Here are a few strategies to help you develop these crucial attributes:

1. **Cultivate a Growth Mindset:** See challenges as growth opportunities, not threats. Learn from your mistakes and failures. They are not a reflection of your worth but stepping stones to success.
2. **Practice Self-Compassion:** Be kind to yourself when you face setbacks or make mistakes. Remember, everyone experiences difficulties. You are not alone in your struggles.
3. **Embrace Change:** Accept that change is a part of life. Instead of resisting it, try to adapt and make the most of new situations.

4. **Build Strong Support Networks:** Surround yourself with positive, supportive people. They can provide advice, encouragement, and a fresh perspective when you face challenges.

Grab your notes app now and jot down a recent situation where you faced a challenge or setback. How did you respond? How can you apply the strategies we've just discussed to show resilience and adaptability in similar situations in the future?

As we move to the final sections of this chapter, remember warrior, resilience, and adaptability are not just skills. They're part of your identity. They shape your journey, fortify your resolve, and illuminate your path towards success.

The Warrior's Meditation — Mental Clarity and Focus

In the rush and chaos of modern life, a barrage of thoughts, distractions, and stressors often fill our minds. A warrior, however, understands the need for mental clarity and focus on navigating the battles of life. Meditation is one of the critical practices warriors use to attain this state of mind. Meditation isn't about turning off your thoughts or trying to achieve a state of eternal calm. Instead, it's about training your mind to focus and redirect your thoughts. It's about observing your thoughts and feelings without judgment and finding inner peace. In addition to promoting mental clarity and focus, regular meditation offers many other benefits. It can reduce stress and anxiety, improve mood and sleep, enhance self-awareness, and increase patience and tolerance.

Incorporating meditation into your daily routine might seem daunting, especially if you're new to the practice. Here are a few steps to start:
1. **Set Aside Time**: Start with just a few minutes each day. Gradually increase the duration as you get more comfortable with the practice.
2. **Find a Quiet Place**: Choose a peaceful environment where you won't be disturbed.
3. **Pay Attention to Your Breath**: Focus on your breath as it goes in and out. If your mind wanders, gently bring it back to your breath.
4. **Be Patient**: Don't worry if you find it difficult at first. The act of bringing your attention back to your breath is the practice of meditation itself.

In your notes app, jot down a time each day when you can practice meditation. Remember, consistency is vital. Even a few minutes each day can make a significant difference.

In the next section, we'll explore another essential aspect of the warrior mindset: gratitude. But for now, take a moment to quiet your mind and feel the stillness within. You're on your way to harnessing the power of the warrior's meditation.

The Power of Gratitude — Cultivating a Positive Mindset

While battles and challenges often mark the life of a warrior, moments of appreciation, gratitude, and joy equally define them. Gratitude is not just about saying thank you. It's a way of seeing the world. It's about shifting your focus from what your life lacks to the present abundance. Cultivating a habit of gratitude has proven benefits. It can improve your physical and psychological health, enhance empathy, reduce aggression, and even help you sleep better. It fosters positivity and pushes you through tough times, reinforcing your warrior mindset.

Here are some ways you can incorporate the power of gratitude into your everyday life:

1. **Keep a Gratitude Journal:** Dedicate a few minutes daily to write down what you're thankful for. They don't have to be big things; small joys count too.
2. **Express Gratitude to Others:** Regularly express your appreciation to the people in your life. Not only will it make them feel good, but it will also increase your awareness of your blessings.
3. **Practice Mindfulness:** Be present and in the moment and appreciate the world around you. During a walk in nature, a quiet moment with a cup of tea, or while enjoying a piece of music.
4. **Use Gratitude Prompts:** If you're having trouble getting started, use prompts such as "Something I'm grateful for in my home is...", "One person I'm thankful for is...", "A happy memory that I'm grateful for is...", and so on.

Open up your notes app and jot down three things you're grateful for. Do this each day, and you'll notice a shift in your mindset and an improvement in your overall well-being.

The next and final section will discuss the importance of rest and recovery in maintaining the warrior mindset. But for now, take a moment to reflect on the abundance in your life and let the power of gratitude strengthen your inner warrior.

Rest and Recovery – Balancing Action and Reflection

The life of a warrior is a constant dance between exertion and rest, action and reflection. Warriors understand that rest is not laziness but a vital part of maintaining strength and endurance. Daily, we glorify busyness and view rest as a luxury or a sign of weakness. However, just as a bow that is always bent will lose its spring, a mind that is always busy will lose its efficiency.

Understanding and respecting your body's need for downtime is essential for physical health, mental clarity, and emotional stability. Moreover, during these moments of quiet reflection, you can evaluate your actions, learn from your experiences, and plan your next steps - reinforcing the strategic aspect of the warrior mindset.

Here's how you can ensure you're giving yourself enough time for rest and recovery:

1. **Prioritise Sleep:** Ensure you're getting enough sleep every night. Sleep is the body's way of healing and restoring itself.
2. **Set Boundaries:** Set clear boundaries between work and rest time. Avoid checking work emails or engaging in work-related activities during your downtime.
3. **Engage in Relaxing Activities:** Engage in activities that help you relax and de-stress. Anything from reading, taking a warm bath, meditating, or sitting quietly.
4. **Practice Mindful Rest:** Be fully present during your rest times. Rather than worrying about your to-do list or ruminating on past events, focus on the here and now.

Open your notes app now and list three restful and relaxing activities. Aim to include at least one of these in your daily routine.

The chapters delve deeper into specific strategies and techniques for developing the warrior mindset. But for now, take some time to rest and reflect on your journey so far. Remember, a true warrior knows when to rest and when to fight.

Chapter 6
Case Studies

Success Stories of the Warrior Mindset

Introduction to Case Studies

When we delve into the annals of history or look around in our world today, we find innumerable instances of individuals who have faced enormous challenges, surmounted seemingly insurmountable odds, and achieved remarkable successes. These individuals have embodied the Warrior Mindset, proving its effectiveness and transformative power. In this chapter, we will look closely at some of these real-life warriors. But why case studies, you may ask? Case studies provide tangible examples of applying the Warrior Mindset in various situations. They are a form of storytelling, and stories have the power to inspire, move, and, most importantly, teach us. Each of these case studies offers a unique perspective on how the principles and strategies of the Warrior Mindset can be applied in real-life circumstances. Moreover, these narratives will make our discussed abstract concepts more tangible and relatable. They also validate the effectiveness of the Warrior Mindset, bringing theory to life and proving that this is not just an abstract concept but a practical tool for life transformation.

Now, pull out your notes app or grab a pen and paper. As you read through these case studies, jot down any insights or strategies that resonate with you. Each story is unique, but they all carry a common thread - The Warrior Mindset.

Your task is to unearth these gems, apply them, and start your transformation journey. Remember, the stories we tell ourselves shape our perception of the world, and perception influences action. By the end of this chapter, I want you to have a collection of stories that inspire you to take action towards becoming a true Warrior.

Case Study 1 - From the Sports Arena: The Warrior Spirit of Serena Williams

When we think about the embodiment of the warrior mindset in the sports arena, it's hard to look past the tennis legend Serena Williams. Serena's journey, from her humble beginnings on the neglected tennis courts of Compton to becoming a global icon, is a testament to the principles of the warrior mindset. Firstly, let's talk about her unwavering belief. Serena and her sister Venus were introduced to tennis by their father at a young age. Despite their socio-economic limitations, the Williams sisters were encouraged to dream big. Serena displayed an unshakeable self-belief that she could rise to the top of a sport far removed from her reality. Another critical element of the warrior mindset Serena has exhibited her relentless preparation. She relentlessly worked on her skills, often practising on the poorly-maintained tennis courts in her neighbourhood, hitting balls until her hands blistered. Serena's ability to embrace the grind, commit to continuous improvement, and withstand the rigours of intense training exemplified her warrior mindset. Serena's story is also one of resilience. In 2003, she experienced a tragedy when her sister was murdered. The incident devastated Serena, but she channelled her grief into her game. Then, after her first child's birth in 2017, Serena faced severe complications that nearly cost her life. Still, she didn't let these adversities break her. Instead, she bounced back stronger, demonstrating her immense resilience and mental toughness. But perhaps the most compelling demonstration of Serena's warrior mindset is her tenacity in adversity. Serena has faced criticism, prejudice, and sexism throughout her career. However, she never let negativity deter her. She stood her ground, displayed remarkable courage, and turned each critique into motivation to better herself both on and off the court. Serena

Williams exemplifies the proper warrior mindset with her indomitable spirit and determination. Her journey serves as an inspiration not only for athletes but for anyone who aspires to overcome challenges, break barriers, and achieve success.

Case Study 2 - The Entrepreneur's Journey: The Warrior Path of Elon Musk

If there's a story of an entrepreneur who has applied the warrior mindset to build successful enterprises from scratch, it's Elon Musk. Known for his roles in creating companies like PayPal, Tesla, SpaceX, and SolarCity, Musk's journey is a case study of the power of the warrior mindset. First and foremost, Musk has shown tremendous courage and vision in the face of uncertainty. Musk took significant risks when investing his fortune in SpaceX and Tesla. He even once stated that he thought both companies would likely fail. But he believed in his mission to make life multi-planetary and transition the world to sustainable energy. He was willing to risk everything for these goals. This boldness to face uncertainty and potential failure is a core element of the warrior mindset. Musk also demonstrates incredible resilience. Both Tesla and SpaceX met near bankruptcy in 2008. But even when defeat seemed inevitable, Musk didn't give up. He remained steadfast, weathered the storm, and ultimately turned the situation around for both companies. The willingness to keep fighting, even in the face of great adversity, is a mark of a true warrior.
Continuous improvement and lifelong learning are hallmarks of Musk's approach. He is known to read widely and deeply across various fields. This curiosity and desire to learn have enabled him to innovate and disrupt multiple industries. When SpaceX was founded, Musk, a self-taught rocket scientist, personally interviewed and questioned the first

employees to ensure they were as committed to learning as he was. Finally, Musk's mental toughness must be noticed. Musk has endured immense stress and pressure from launch failures, production issues, and public scrutiny. Yet, he remains dedicated and continues to push towards his vision. His ability to survive and stay focused under pressure is a testament to his mental toughness. Musk's journey has controversy and criticism. However, his success story exemplifies the warrior mindset at work in entrepreneurship. His vision, resilience, commitment to improvement, and mental toughness have propelled him to remarkable heights and continue to drive him towards even more audacious goals.

Case Study 3 - Transformation Through Personal Adversity: The Resilient Spirit of Nick Vujicic

Nick Vujicic's story is one of immense personal adversity and an inspiring demonstration of the warrior mindset. Born without limbs due to a rare condition known as tetra-amelia syndrome, Vujicic's early life was filled with challenges, discrimination, and despair. However, he used his adversity as a platform to cultivate the warrior mindset and not only cope with his situation but also thrive and inspire millions worldwide. From an early age, Vujicic had to confront his fears and push past his comfort zones. He learned to do everyday tasks such as brushing his teeth, typing on a computer, and even swimming without limbs, demonstrating extraordinary courage. Resilience is another hallmark of the warrior mindset, and Vujicic has it in abundance. Despite being bullied and isolated as a child and grappling with severe depression and suicidal thoughts, he found the strength to persevere. He turned his personal adversity into an opportunity to inspire others, becoming a motivational speaker who travels worldwide, sharing his story and empowering others to overcome their challenges. Vujicic also embodies the principle of continuous learning and improvement. Faced with physical limitations that would seem insurmountable to most, he learned to adapt and find new ways to function and thrive. Despite his condition, his ability to perform physical tasks and lead an independent life attests to his relentless pursuit of growth and self-improvement.

Furthermore, Vujicic exemplifies mental toughness. Instead of allowing his physical condition to define his life, he redefined what was possible, refusing to let his limitations confine his ambitions. He completed his tertiary education, authored several best-selling books, and even started a non-profit organisation. Vujicic's life is a powerful testament to the power of the warrior mindset. Despite his extraordinary circumstances, he adopted the principles of courage, resilience, continuous learning, and mental toughness, transforming personal adversity into a journey of empowerment and impact. His story reminds us that we can turn our struggles into strength and trials into triumphs with the right mindset.

Case Study 4 - The Military Veteran: Transitioning Successfully into Civilian Life

Meet Jack, a decorated military veteran who served for over two decades in various high-pressure situations on and off the battlefield. When it was time for him to retire and transition into civilian life, the journey wasn't without challenges. Adjusting to a slower pace, finding a job that matched his unique skill set, and reconnecting with his family full-time required a significant shift. But Jack was not unfamiliar with adversity; he had his warrior mindset to lean on, a perspective cultivated over years of military service. Firstly, Jack applied the principle of goal-setting that he had learned in his military training. Jack identified what he wanted to achieve in his civilian life - a fulfilling job where Jack could utilise his leadership skills, quality time with his family, and continuous personal growth. He used the SMART criteria, ensuring his goals were Specific, Measurable, Achievable, Relevant, and Time-bound.

Next, Jack created a detailed strategic plan to reach his goals. He analysed his strengths and areas of improvement, adapted his military skills to suit civilian life, and explored various career options. Jack broke down his main goal into smaller, manageable tasks, each with a specific timeline. This strategic planning was something he'd executed countless times during missions, and it served him well in his new venture. Embracing the warrior mindset principle of resilience, Jack persevered even when he faced rejection in job interviews. Jack viewed every rejection as an opportunity to learn, grow, and adapt his approach. He networked relentlessly, sought guidance from mentors, and leveraged resources designed to assist veterans transitioning into the civilian workforce. His discipline and consistency, traits honed in the military, were instrumental in maintaining his physical and mental health during this transition. Jack kept a strict routine for physical exercise, something he'd always done during his military service. He also incorporated mindfulness practices into his training to maintain mental fitness. Jack's story is a testament to how the warrior mindset's principles, learned on the battlefield, can be successfully applied to civilian life. His journey, from his military career to his smooth transition into civilian life, illustrates how the warrior mindset can lead to success in any arena of life. Jack's experience serves as a potent reminder that the warrior mindset isn't restricted to the battlefield; it's a mindset for life.

Case Study 5 - The Activist Making a Difference: The Undaunted Spirit of Malala Yousafzai

Malala Yousafzai, the Pakistani activist for girls' education, embodies the warrior mindset in every sense. Her life, punctuated by extraordinary courage, resilience, self-belief, and perseverance, is an inspirational tale of fighting against societal constraints to bring about change. Growing up in Swat Valley, Pakistan, Malala was exposed to the harsh realities of gender discrimination early on. The Taliban, an extremist group, had taken control of the region and imposed strict rules, including banning girls from attending school. Despite the life-threatening risks, Malala, driven by courage, a vital principle of the warrior mindset, stood against this unjust decree. She started a blog under a pseudonym, sharing her life under Taliban rule and her desire for education, thus revealing an extraordinary level of bravery. Resilience is another component of the warrior mindset. Malala exemplified this trait when she survived an assassination attempt by the Taliban. The incident strengthened her resolve and galvanised global support for her cause. She used this moment not to retreat but to amplify her voice for girls' education, symbolising incredible tenacity and resilience. Continuous learning and self-improvement, crucial to the warrior mindset, are also integral to Malala's story. Despite the adverse circumstances, Malala remained a voracious learner. After moving to the UK for treatment and safety, she continued her education, performed exceptionally well academically, and studied at the University of Oxford, demonstrating her commitment to learning. Despite the immense challenges and threats she faced, Malala's mental toughness, a critical warrior mindset trait, is evident in her consistent advocacy for girls' education. Her unwavering focus and determination led to the establishment of the Malala Fund, aimed at breaking down barriers to girls' education worldwide. In recognition of her struggle and contribution to children's rights, Malala became the youngest recipient of the Nobel Peace Prize at age 17, a testament to her strong sense of purpose and self-belief, crucial aspects of the warrior mindset. Through her journey, Malala Yousafzai demonstrates the power of the warrior mindset to overcome societal obstacles and effect change. Her story stands as a beacon of inspiration for anyone battling adversity, reminding us that we can shape our destiny and impact the world with unwavering determination and the right mindset.

Case Study Analysis and Common Themes

Analysing the cases of the athlete, the entrepreneur, the military veteran, the individual who faced immense personal adversity, and the activist, we can extract many vital takeaways and common themes related to the warrior mindset.

1. **Courage and Bravery:** All individuals in our case studies faced significant challenges or adversity. From the athlete dealing with tough competition and potentially career-ending injuries, the entrepreneur braving the odds and facing the uncertainty of the business world, the veteran transitioning from a military to a civilian environment, the individual dealing with personal adversity, to Malala standing against societal norms and threats, courage was a common trait. They had the bravery to face their fears, confront their

realities, and take calculated risks, thus embodying the essence of the warrior mindset.
2. **Resilience and Adaptability:** Each case also highlighted resilience and adaptability, essential elements of the warrior mindset. Whether the athlete bouncing back from defeat, the entrepreneur learning from failures, the veteran adapting to a completely different lifestyle, the individual healing from personal loss, or Malala recovering from a life-threatening attack, they all exemplify the quality of resilience. They faced obstacles, endured, learned, adapted, and emerged stronger, embodying the warrior mindset.
3. **Self-Belief and Determination:** All our subjects displayed immense self-belief and determination. The athlete believed in his talent and potential, the entrepreneur in her unique idea and business acumen, the veteran in his skills and discipline, the individual facing adversity in their ability to overcome, and Malala in her cause and power to bring about change. Their unwavering determination drove them to persevere and achieve their goals.
4. **Purpose and Vision:** A strong sense of purpose and a clear vision were instrumental in all these stories. A clear goal or purpose provides the motivation and direction to channel their efforts effectively. It fueled their warrior mindset, enabling them to overcome challenges and keep moving forward.
5. **Continuous Learning and Self-Improvement:** Each case also demonstrated the importance of continuous learning and self-improvement, vital elements of the warrior mindset. Our subjects were lifelong learners who continually sought to improve themselves by refining their skills, gaining new knowledge, understanding their weaknesses, or seeking constructive feedback.

In conclusion, these case studies offer invaluable insights into applying the warrior mindset in various facets of life. They demonstrate how courage, resilience, self-belief, a strong sense of purpose, and a commitment to continuous learning can empower individuals to overcome adversity, achieve their goals, and bring about meaningful change.

Lessons for the Reader

The case studies we've explored are stories of extraordinary individuals and lessons of resilience, determination, and the power of the warrior mindset. Here's what you, as a reader, can take away from these stories:

1. **Courage is Non-Negotiable:** In adversity or uncertainty, courage is your greatest ally. But remember, courage doesn't mean the absence of fear - it's the decision that something else is more important than fear. In your life, embrace the unknown, take calculated risks, and be courageous in pursuing your goals.
2. **Develop Resilience:** Resilience is about returning from setbacks and adapting to change. Life will inevitably present you with challenges, but your ability to recover just adapt defines your strength. Cultivate resilience by looking at failures and setbacks as opportunities for learning and growth.
3. **Believe in Yourself:** Self-belief can move mountains. Trust in your abilities and maintain your resolve in the face of adversity. This doesn't mean ignoring your weaknesses; instead, acknowledge them and work on improving them.
4. **Find Your Purpose:** A strong sense of purpose can be a powerful driving force. Use it as a compass to guide your actions and decisions. It could be anything from a career goal, a personal ambition, or a cause you deeply care about.

5. **Never Stop Learning:** The most successful people are lifelong learners. Continually seek opportunities to gain new knowledge, develop skills, and expand your mindset. Embrace feedback, even when critical, and use it to better yourself.
6. **The Warrior Mindset is Accessible to All:** Regardless of the circumstance, anyone can cultivate a warrior mindset - it's not reserved for the select few. It's a matter of choice and commitment.

From these case studies, it's clear that the warrior mindset can be instrumental in achieving success and overcoming adversity. The next time you face a challenge, big or small. Invoke the warrior within you and face the situation head-on. You are more powerful than you think.

Conclusion

Throughout this chapter, we've journeyed through real-life narratives, stories of triumph, resilience, and the indomitable power of the human spirit. These aren't merely tales; they are testaments to the transformative power of the warrior mindset. These case studies - the athlete who defied all odds, the entrepreneur who built an empire from nothing, the individual who blossomed in the face of personal adversity, the veteran who successfully transitioned into civilian life, and the activist who effectuated societal change - are different paths on the same map, connected by the common thread of the warrior mindset. Each individual faced unique challenges, but the warrior mindset enabled them to navigate their hardships and emerge victorious. Their stories exemplify what is possible when courage, resilience, belief, purpose, and the quest for learning are at the helm. As we conclude this chapter, remember that these stories are not exclusive to the extraordinary. The warrior mindset isn't a gift bestowed upon a chosen few; it's a choice, a way of life accessible to all of us. These stories mirror our potential, reflecting what we can achieve when we embrace the principles of the warrior mindset. Whether you're an entrepreneur, a professional, a student, or trying to make positive changes, the warrior mindset is your secret weapon. It's the bridge between where you are and want to be. As you turn the page, remember the lessons learned from these warriors. Let their journeys inspire you and, more importantly, remind you of your strength. In each of us resides a warrior, waiting to rise when summoned. So, here's to the warriors - the ones who are and those in the making. Harness the power of the warrior mindset, and become the hero of your own story. There's no more fitting way to conclude than by echoing the words of the ancient philosopher Marcus Aurelius: "You have power over your mind - not outside events. Realise this, and you will find strength."

Chapter 7

The Warrior Mindset in Everyday Life

Putting it All Together

Introduction

As we dive into this chapter, I want to share something crucial that might surprise you: the warrior mindset isn't just for the battlefield or the sports arena, the boardroom or the gym. It isn't reserved solely for when we're up against seemingly insurmountable challenges or tackling herculean tasks. In fact, the true power of the warrior mindset lies in its application to everyday life. Yes, you heard it right, daily life - from the moment you rise in the morning to the moment you lay down to rest at night. This includes your interactions with your family, daily work, personal habits, health, goals - everything. Remember that extraordinary lives are not built from extraordinary moments alone. They are constructed from the thousands of ordinary moments we experience daily. What we choose to do in these moments that determines the quality and direction of our lives. And it's in these seemingly mundane moments that the warrior mindset truly comes into play. Adopting this mindset in all aspects of life, you can live more fully, authentically, and bravely. You can navigate challenges with grace, pursue your goals with relentless determination, and build a life that is true to your highest self. Now, let's dive in and see how you can bring the warrior mindset into every facet of your life.

The Warrior Mindset in Personal Life

When we think of warriors, we often imagine them in the heat of battle or during a critical mission. But what about when the warrior takes off their armour, so to speak? How does the warrior mindset inform their personal life, relationships, the pursuit of health and wellness, and their ongoing journey of personal growth? For starters, let's consider the family dynamic. Like the battlefield, family relationships can be complex and fraught with challenges.

Differences of opinion, clashes in personality, and past hurts can all lead to tension and conflict. Here, the warrior mindset offers us a way forward. It enables us to face these difficulties head-on, to communicate openly and honestly, and to seek resolution instead of victory. It reminds us that our loved ones aren't our adversaries but our allies, each with strengths, weaknesses, and perspectives. When it comes to maintaining health and wellness, the warrior mindset is invaluable.

Consider the discipline of a warrior training for combat. They don't skip workouts or indulge in unhealthy habits that could compromise their readiness. They understand that their physical condition directly impacts their ability to perform under pressure. Similarly, we can apply this same discipline to our own health routines, pushing ourselves to exercise regularly, eat healthily, and prioritise rest. This isn't about striving for perfection or punishing ourselves when we fall short. It's about valuing our bodies and minds, treating them with the care they deserve, and recognising that our overall wellness contributes to our quality of life. Finally, the journey of personal development is where the warrior mindset truly shines. As warriors, we understand that growth isn't a destination but a continual process. We embrace the challenges and obstacles we face as opportunities for learning and improvement. We persist in facing failure and adversity, knowing that each setback is a stepping stone to becoming our best selves. Now, take a moment to reflect on your own personal life. Where can you start implementing the warrior mindset? Are there relationships that need your attention? Could you make healthier choices for your physical well-being? What step can you take today on your journey of personal development?

Go on, jot down some thoughts in your notes app. Remember, it's not about making radical changes overnight. It's about taking small, consistent steps towards cultivating the warrior mindset in your everyday life.

The Warrior Mindset in Professional Life

Transitioning from our personal life to our professional one, applying the warrior mindset remains equally critical, if not more so. Let's delve into how these principles can help us in our work environment, whether it's goal setting, managing stress, leading a team, or being a more effective member of an organisation. Goal setting is an integral part of any professional endeavour. It gives us a clear direction and helps us align our actions towards achieving these objectives. But setting the goal is just the start. The warrior mindset enables us to pursue these objectives with relentless determination and resilience. We do not shy away from obstacles. Instead, we see them as opportunities to strengthen our resolve and adapt our strategies. Next, let's consider work stress. As inevitable as it may be, excessive stress can lead to burnout and severely impact our performance. A warrior understands the importance of managing stress effectively. They do not let stress overwhelm them. Instead, they leverage it as a motivator, using it to fuel their drive and focus. Mindfulness practices, physical exercise, and regular breaks are just a few ways to manage our stress levels, just as a warrior would. If you're in a position of leading a team or aspire to be, the warrior mindset offers invaluable insights. A good leader, much like a good warrior, is not just strong but also empathetic. They understand their team member's strengths and weaknesses and know how to leverage them effectively. They communicate openly, listen actively, and inspire their team towards a common goal. They lead by example, showcasing the warrior mindset in action. Even as individual contributors, the warrior mindset allows us to become more effective members of our organisation. It cultivates a sense of responsibility, professionalism, and a commitment to continual learning and improvement. Now, consider your own professional life. How can you incorporate the warrior mindset into your work? What goals could you set and pursue with the warrior's tenacity? How can you better manage your work stress? If you're a leader, how can you inspire the warrior mindset in your team? If not, how can you use it to contribute more effectively to your organisation?

Take a moment to reflect on these questions, and jot down your thoughts and actions in your notes app. Remember, cultivating the warrior mindset is a journey, not a destination. Small, consistent steps can lead to significant changes over time.

Applying the Warrior Mindset to Overcome Everyday Challenges

Life is riddled with challenges, big and small, expected and unexpected. But through the lens of a warrior mindset, these are not obstacles but growth opportunities. Let's explore how the principles of this mindset can help us face and conquer everyday problems.

1. **Traffic and Commuting Stress:** So many of us commute countless hours every week. It's easy to view this time as wasted, causing stress and frustration. But if we apply the warrior mindset, we can turn this around. We can use this time as an opportunity to develop patience and resilience. Listening to audiobooks or podcasts can turn commuting into a learning experience. Practising mindfulness can turn it into a moment of peace before and after a hectic day.
2. **Health and Fitness:** Staying healthy and fit is a common challenge. The warrior mindset encourages

discipline, persistence, and resilience, essential for maintaining a regular fitness routine. Even when progress seems slow, it teaches us to celebrate small victories and remain committed to our goals.
3. **Interpersonal Conflict:** Whether at home or work, conflicts are inevitable. Instead of escalating or avoiding the situation, the warrior mindset pushes us to face the issue head-on, listen empathetically, and honestly communicate our feelings and needs. This not only resolves the conflict but also strengthens the relationship.
4. **Personal Finance Management:** Managing personal finances can be overwhelming. A warrior, however, takes charge of their financial health. They set clear financial goals, create budgets, track expenses, and take conscious steps to increase their financial literacy. They face economic challenges with courage, taking calculated risks when necessary.
5. **Public Speaking** is a common fear, but the warrior mindset helps us tackle it. Viewing it as a skill to be mastered rather than a fear to be avoided, we can gradually increase our comfort level through practice and preparation. Each time we speak publicly, we build confidence and improve.

Reflect upon your own everyday challenges. How can you apply the warrior mindset to overcome them?

What small steps can you take today that will contribute to your growth as a warrior? Jot down your reflections and action steps in your notes app, and remember, the real progress lies in the journey, not just the destination.

Mindfulness and the Warrior Mindset

At its core, mindfulness is being fully present and engaged in the current moment, aware of our thoughts, feelings, and actions without judgment. It's akin to the quiet before the battle, the moment a warrior takes to centre themselves before charging into the fray. But how does mindfulness tie into the warrior mindset, and how can it enhance our ability to use this mindset effectively in everyday life? Let's explore.

1. Enhanced Awareness: Mindfulness enhances our self-awareness. It helps us become more cognizant of our thoughts, emotions, and behaviours, allowing us to identify patterns and areas we need to work on. Just as a warrior needs to know their strengths and weaknesses to strategise effectively, so do we in our daily lives.
2. Emotional Control: Mindfulness helps us regulate our emotions. It teaches us not to suppress or react impulsively to our feelings but to acknowledge and understand them. This emotional control is a fundamental aspect of the warrior mindset. By maintaining control, we respond rather than react, make thoughtful decisions, and avoid unnecessary conflict.
3. Presence: Being fully present is a cornerstone of mindfulness and the warrior mindset. In the middle of the battle, a warrior cannot afford to dwell on the past or worry about the future; they must be entirely present. Similarly, in everyday life, being present enhances our interactions with others and our work's quality and enjoyment.
4. Stress Management: Mindfulness is an effective stress management tool. Regular practice reduces cortisol levels, improves sleep, and enhances overall well-being. A warrior who cannot manage stress will not succeed on the battlefield. The same applies in life. The warrior

mindset and mindfulness give us the tools to handle stress healthily.
5. Acceptance and Compassion: Mindfulness teaches us to meet ourselves and others with acceptance and compassion. This isn't about being soft or weak but about understanding that we're all human, all fighting our battles. This understanding helps us to be patient with ourselves and others, a trait inherent in the warrior mindset.

To cultivate mindfulness, start small. Dedicate a few minutes daily to silence, focusing on your breath or surroundings. There are numerous mindfulness apps available to guide you through this process.

Write down your experiences and observations in your notes app, and with regular practice, you'll start to notice a shift towards a more mindful and warrior-like approach to life.

Building Resilience with the Warrior Mindset

Resilience - it's a term we often hear thrown around when discussing the ability to bounce back from adversity. It is the capacity to recover quickly from difficulties and spring back into shape. So, how does the warrior mindset contribute to building this invaluable trait, and why is it essential in our lives?

The warrior mindset and resilience are intimately intertwined, influencing and reinforcing the other. Here's how:

1. **Adaptability:** Adapting to changing circumstances is vital to the warrior mindset. It's about seeing the battlefield's shifting terrain, understanding the modifications, and adjusting strategies accordingly. In life, this adaptability translates into resilience. It allows

us to navigate through the ups and downs, the unexpected twists and turns, with grace and agility.
2. **Overcoming Fear:** The warrior mindset equips us with the courage to face our fears head-on. Instead of avoiding challenging situations, we learn to meet them directly, strengthening our mental and emotional muscles. Like a warrior in battle, the more we face our fears, the less power they have over us, bolstering our resilience over time.
3. **Embracing Failure:** A warrior knows that not every battle will be won. But losing a fight doesn't make them any less of a warrior. They see each failure as a lesson, an opportunity for growth. This mindset, when applied in our lives, enhances our resilience. We learn to see failures not as the end but as stepping stones to success.
4. **Self-Belief:** At the heart of the warrior mindset is an unshakable belief in oneself. This belief isn't rooted in arrogance but a deep understanding of one's abilities and potential. This self-belief is powerful armour, protecting us from criticism, self-doubt, and setbacks, making us more resilient.
5. **Endurance:** A warrior understands the importance of endurance. They know that battles are not always won by the swift but by those who keep going when everything seems lost. This ability to endure and to keep moving forward even when things are tough is a crucial element of resilience.

Why is this important? Life, as we know, is full of challenges. Resilience means facing these challenges with strength and perseverance without losing our sense of self or purpose. It allows us to maintain our mental health and progress towards our goals, no matter what life throws. Cultivating a warrior mindset is about thriving in extraordinary circumstances and becoming more resilient in our everyday lives.

Making the Warrior Mindset a Habit

Much like any new skill, the warrior mindset must be practised consistently to take root and become a part of our lives. The goal is to make the warrior mindset not just something we do but who we are - an integral part of our character. But how do we do this? How do we ensure that we consistently apply the principles of the warrior mindset, thus making it a habit? Here are some tips on how to incorporate the warrior mindset into your daily routine and create practices that support it:

1. **Set Clear Goals**: Warriors always have a clear mission or goal. In the context of your personal and professional life, this translates to setting clear and attainable goals. When you know what you're striving towards, it's easier to maintain focus and determination, critical attributes of the warrior mindset.
2. **Daily Affirmations**: Start your day with affirmations that reinforce the warrior mindset. Phrases like "I am resilient," "I can face any challenge that comes my way," or "I believe in my abilities" can help instil the mindset at the start of each day.
3. **Mindfulness Practice**: As we've discussed, mindfulness is a crucial component of the warrior mindset. Incorporate a daily mindfulness practice into your routine, whether meditation, mindful walking, or simply taking a few minutes each day to sit quietly and focus on your breath.
4. **Embrace Challenges**: Make it a habit to regularly step outside your comfort zone. This could mean trying something new, tackling a difficult task, or facing fear.

The more you practice overcoming challenges, the more natural the warrior mindset becomes.
5. **Reflection**: At the end of each day, take some time to reflect on how you've applied the warrior mindset. What challenges did you face, and how did you handle them? This daily reflection can help you identify areas of growth and places where you've excelled.
6. **Physical Fitness**: A warrior takes care of their body and mind. Regular physical activity, whether going to the gym, taking a yoga class, or running, promotes physical health, mental toughness, and resilience.
7. **Continuous Learning**: A true warrior never stops learning. Make it a habit to constantly seek knowledge and new experiences. This can help you adapt to new situations and keep your mind sharp and focused.

Remember, the warrior mindset is not an overnight transformation. It takes time, patience, and consistent practice. But by incorporating these habits into your daily routine, you're one step closer to living with a true warrior's resilience, courage, and determination.

Summary and Key Takeaways

This chapter aimed to bring the warrior mindset into our daily lives, demonstrating its applicability and immense potential in everyday personal and professional situations. It's not just for overcoming extraordinary obstacles or for dramatic transformations. Instead, the warrior mindset can guide us in navigating daily challenges, making decisions, building resilience, and leading a fulfilling and meaningful life. Here are the key takeaways from this chapter:

1. **Applicability in Personal Life**: The warrior mindset is crucial in our lives, helping us maintain healthy

relationships, invest in self-care and personal development, and handle emotional challenges.
2. **Importance in Professional Life**: In the professional world, the warrior mindset guides goal setting, stress management, team leadership, and effective decision-making.
3. **Overcoming Everyday Challenges**: The warrior mindset is not just for monumental battles but also for our daily struggles. It provides a framework to effectively approach, face, and overcome these challenges.
4. **Mindfulness and the Warrior Mindset**: Mindfulness is an integral part of the warrior mindset, enabling us to stay focused, aware, and present in every situation. It helps maintain the equilibrium necessary to act according to the principles of the warrior mindset.
5. **Building Resilience**: The warrior mindset contributes significantly to building personal resilience. It helps us bounce back from setbacks, adapt to change, and maintain a positive outlook.
6. **Making it a Habit**: Incorporating the warrior mindset into your daily routine requires setting clear goals, practising daily affirmations, embracing challenges, nurturing physical fitness, and engaging in continuous learning. It's all about making it a part of your identity, which requires consistent practice and commitment.

Remember, the warrior mindset is a journey, not a destination. It's about embracing the process, learning from every experience, and striving to improve daily. It's about turning adversity into opportunity and living a life of courage, resilience, and determination. This is the true power of the warrior mindset in everyday life.

Conclusion

And here we are, after this transformative journey through the landscape of the warrior mindset. We started with understanding the concept and its origins. We now arrived at how you can apply it in your everyday life. It's been quite a journey, hasn't it?

This mindset isn't just about preparing for significant battles or transformative moments. It's about the small decisions we make daily, the challenges we face, and the opportunities we encounter. It's about our relationships, work, health, and happiness. Essentially, it's about life. In our personal lives, the warrior mindset teaches us to foster more robust, healthier relationships and invest in self-care and personal growth. It helps us navigate emotional difficulties and face life's curveballs with courage and resilience. In the professional realm, this mindset guides us in setting and achieving goals, managing stress, leading teams, and making effective decisions. It equips us to excel in our careers, not just survive them. And in everyday challenges, the warrior mindset becomes our compass, helping us face and overcome obstacles with strength, patience, and determination. But it's important to remember that developing and maintaining the warrior mindset is not an event but a process. It requires consistent practice, patience, and a commitment to personal growth. However, the payoff is enormous. By embracing the warrior mindset, you're setting yourself up for success, resilience, fulfilment, and inner peace. It empowers you to become the best version of yourself and lead a life that aligns with your values and aspirations.

As we close this chapter and you step into the arena of life, remember to carry the warrior mindset with you. Make it your shield against adversity, your sword against complacency, and your beacon towards success. And as you do, remember that the warrior within you is more potent than any challenge you will ever face. Embrace, nurture, and let it guide you to your highest potential. Here's to the warrior in you. May you face every challenge with courage, every failure with resilience, and every success with humility. Keep moving forward, keep growing, and remember - the warrior's journey is lifelong, but so are its rewards.

Chapter 8

Warrior Mindset in Different Cultures

Introduction

Welcome back, dear reader. We're now diving into a new, exciting dimension of the warrior mindset - its cultural manifestations. Have you ever wondered how universal the warrior mindset is? Well, it's time to shed light on this fascinating question. As we've discussed, the warrior mindset is all about courage, resilience, discipline, adaptability, and a commitment to growth. It's about facing life's battles head-on and growing stronger. But does this mindset translate across cultural boundaries? The answer is a resounding yes. A warrior's ethos is woven into the fabric of human history and culture. Across continents and throughout different eras, human societies have revered the principles we've been exploring in this book. The warrior mindset has manifested itself in many ways, shaped by other societies' unique cultures, values, and circumstances. However, despite these variations, a powerful commonality binds these manifestations together - the universal human pursuit of resilience, growth, and personal mastery. In this chapter, we're going on a journey worldwide and back in time. We'll explore how the warrior mindset has been interpreted and embraced by various cultures, from the samurai of Japan to the Spartans of Ancient Greece and the indigenous cultures across the globe. In each instance, we'll uncover the specific expressions of the warrior mindset and draw lessons that are just as relevant today as they were centuries ago.

The Samurai of Japan

We start our cultural exploration in the Land of the Rising Sun, where the samurai class exemplified a unique version of the warrior mindset. Samurai, the military nobility of medieval and early-modern Japan, were not just warriors known for their martial prowess but also embodiments of refined culture and philosophy. Central to their way of life was 'Bushido', translated as 'The Way of the Warrior.' Bushido was a moral code of conduct that governed a samurai's life, placing great importance on virtues like rectitude, courage, benevolence, respect, honesty, honour, and loyalty. The samurai were expected to fearlessly face adversity and display unyielding loyalty to their masters while cultivating wisdom, artistic sensibilities, and a deep appreciation for the fleeting nature of life. Can you see the parallels to the modern warrior mindset? As we have been discussing, the samurai embraced courage not just on the battlefield but in every aspect of their lives. They valued discipline, honed their skills diligently, and committed to continual learning and growth. Benevolence, respect, and honesty underscored their interactions with others, reflecting the importance of emotional intelligence and empathy in the warrior mindset. The principle of loyalty speaks to the warrior's sense of purpose and commitment - a commitment to a cause, dedication to others, and, above all, commitment to their personal growth and moral code. The samurai also had a deep awareness of life's impermanence, a concept captured by the phrase 'mono no aware' (the pathos of things). This mindfulness of life's transience sharpened their focus on the present moment. It spurred them to live each day to the fullest - a principle that resonates with our earlier discussions on mindfulness. So, from the samurai, we learn a powerful lesson: the warrior mindset is not just about facing life's battles but about how we live between them. It's about living with purpose, integrity, and a deep appreciation for life's journey. And these are lessons we can carry with us, regardless of the battles we face in our own lives.

The Spartans of Ancient Greece

Let's journey now to the rugged landscapes of Ancient Greece, to the city-state of Sparta, renowned for its military might and warrior culture. Spartans provide another fascinating study of the warrior mindset. Although their society vastly differed from the samurai's, some core elements of the warrior mindset were remarkably similar. From childhood, the Spartans were known for their rigorous training regimen to forge strong warriors and citizens. The system, known as the 'agoge,' was a test of discipline, endurance, and resilience, instilling a sense of duty, courage, and community in each Spartan. Discipline was at the heart of Spartan life. They adhered to a strict daily routine and were trained to maintain composure and control in all circumstances. This disciplined lifestyle is a striking example of one aspect of the warrior mindset - the importance of self-control and consistent practice in honing one's skills and character. Resilience was another critical aspect of the Spartan warrior mindset. From a young age, Spartans were conditioned to endure hardship without complaint. They were taught to accept life's challenges as opportunities for growth. This concept aligns perfectly with our discussion on the role of adversity in shaping the warrior mindset. Lastly, the Spartans had a profound sense of service and community. Their training and lifestyle were aimed not just at personal glory but at the collective well-being of Sparta. They stood together, fought together, and died when necessary. This deep sense of collective duty and service is an essential aspect of the warrior mindset - the understanding that our battles are not just about us but the greater good. While Spartan society had its flaws and is far removed from our modern world, the principles of discipline, resilience, and service resonate with us today. They provide valuable insights into living the warrior mindset - remaining disciplined in our pursuits, resilient in the face of challenges, and committed to serving something greater than ourselves.

The Vikings of Scandinavia

Our next stop takes us to the chilly fjords of Scandinavia, where we explore the warrior mindset as it was embodied by the Vikings. Known for their adventurous spirit, fierceness in battle, and robust sense of personal honour, the Vikings provide another perspective on the warrior mindset. The Viking ethos was deeply rooted in bravery. Warriors were expected to show courage in the face of danger, not just in battle but in every aspect of their lives. This valour was not about reckless risk-taking but about facing life's challenges with audacity and determination. This aligns with our understanding of the warrior mindset, where courage plays a central role in overcoming external obstacles and conquering our inner fears and insecurities. The adventure was another defining characteristic of the Vikings. Their expeditions across the seas are well-documented and have become the stuff of legends. This adventurous spirit speaks to a fundamental aspect of the warrior mindset - the willingness to step out of comfort zones, explore the unknown, and constantly seek growth. Just as the Vikings ventured out into unfamiliar seas, we must be willing to take risks and embrace new experiences to expand our horizons and grow. Lastly, personal honour was a cornerstone of the Viking culture. A Viking's honour was tied to their actions and their conduct among their peers. They were expected to be honest, reliable, and to stand by their word - a concept known as 'dróttins níð,' or 'lord's disgrace,' emphasised the shame of failing to live up to one's word. This focus on personal honour and integrity directly ties into the warrior mindset. Being true to ourselves, keeping our promises, and maintaining our integrity is integral to the warrior mindset. In the Viking culture, we see how bravery, the spirit of adventure, and a sense of personal honour come together to form a unique expression of the warrior mindset - one that still has much to teach us in the present day. Whether embarking on an exciting new project or endeavouring to live with integrity and courage, we can draw inspiration from the Vikings as we navigate our paths.

Indigenous Cultures

As we continue our global journey, let's shift our focus to some of the world's indigenous cultures. While there are countless diverse indigenous communities, many share common threads of deep respect for the land, community strength, and storytelling's power - elements that contribute to their unique expression of the warrior mindset. This section will highlight two communities: the Maori of New Zealand and the Native American warriors of North America. Starting with the Maori people of New Zealand, we see a robust tradition of warrior culture. The Haka, a traditional Maori dance, is one of the most well-known representations of this. Performed before battles, the Haka displayed strength, prowess, and a means to invoke the gods and ancestors for support. Central to Maori warrior culture is "mana," a term encompassing authority, charisma, and spiritual power.

Maintaining and enhancing one's mana through courage, wisdom, and humility aligns with the values we've been exploring in the warrior mindset. Turning our attention to Native American cultures, we find a rich tapestry of warrior traditions. While diverse, many Native American tribes revered their warriors for their physical strength and wisdom, integrity, and commitment to their people. Warriors were seen as protectors, responsible for the well-being of their tribe. This role required physical strength, emotional resilience, strategic thinking, and strong moral character – elements that resonate deeply with the principles of the warrior mindset we've been discussing. They cultivated a sense of harmony with nature and their surroundings. This mindfulness is a crucial part of the warrior mindset. In the Maori and Native American cultures, being a warrior goes beyond physical prowess. It involves a deep connection with the spiritual and natural world, a commitment to community, and the cultivation of personal virtues. These values reflect the essence of the warrior mindset and offer us valuable insights into incorporating these principles into our lives.

The Shaolin Monks of China

As we further explore the manifestations of the warrior mindset around the world, let's travel to the ancient temples of China and examine the Shaolin monks' unique approach. These monks are famous for their profound spiritual practice intertwined with martial arts mastery, which provides an intriguing lens through which to view the warrior mindset. Shaolin Kung Fu, a martial art developed within the Shaolin monasteries of China, is a physical manifestation of the monks' philosophy and spiritual practice. At first glance, the rigorous physical discipline, precision, and strength of Shaolin Kung Fu are the primary indicators of the warrior mindset. However, these physical attributes are just the surface of a much deeper philosophy. Fundamental to the Shaolin approach is the principle of Zen or Chan Buddhism. This philosophy emphasises mindfulness, intuition, and the cultivation of a peaceful mind amidst life's adversities. The Shaolin monks seek to unify the body, mind, and spirit through their practices, manifesting a comprehensive warrior mindset far beyond physical combat. The ability to stay centred, even in the face of intense physical demands or potential danger, represents an essential aspect of the warrior mindset. From the Shaolin monks, we learn that being a warrior is not just about the ability to fight. Instead, it is about remaining calm, focused, and mindful. It is about cultivating inner peace and resilience, which enables one to respond effectively to life's challenges. As such, the Shaolin monks offer us a profound lesson in integrating physical discipline with mental and spiritual cultivation. Their philosophy and practices provide yet another model for developing and embodying the warrior mindset in our lives.

Similarities and Differences

As we have traversed across continents and through time, exploring the warrior mindset through various cultural lenses, it becomes evident that while each culture embodies unique characteristics, they also share common threads.

Similarities:

Across all cultures, the warrior mindset embodies resilience, discipline, honour, and courage. Whether it's the samurai's disciplined life, the Vikings' bravery, the Spartans' resilience, the honour among indigenous warriors, or the mental mastery of the Shaolin monks - each warrior culture emphasises these core principles. Another common thread is the practice of rigorous physical training, often coupled with mental and spiritual disciplines. Moreover, each culture instils a sense of purpose and service in its warriors. They are seen not only as individuals who engage in combat but also as protectors of their communities and upholders of their cultural values.

Differences:

While these core principles are shared across the cultures we've examined, how they manifest these values can vary significantly. For instance, the emphasis on community service and personal sacrifice is more pronounced in the samurai's Bushido code and the Spartan lifestyle. On the other hand, the Viking warrior ethos places a higher value on personal courage and the quest for glory. The Shaolin monks stand apart in their unique integration of martial skills with deep spiritual practice, which embodies their warrior mindset. Such differences reflect the diverse cultural contexts in which these warrior mindsets evolved. These contexts influenced not just the behaviours and beliefs of the warriors themselves but also the broader societies they were part of. In exploring these similarities and differences, we gain a deeper understanding of the universal principles underpinning the warrior mindset. At the same time, we appreciate the unique ways these principles can be expressed, offering a rich tapestry of examples to draw inspiration for our journeys.

Lessons for the Reader

It's quite the journey we've embarked on, isn't it? We have travelled across time, continents, and cultures, delving into warriors' ethos from the pages of history. But what can we, modern-day readers, gather from these historical and cultural examples of the warrior mindset?

- Resilience: We learned from the Spartans the true essence of resilience. It isn't about not experiencing hardship or failure, but rather, it's about getting back up each time we fall. It's about facing adversity head-on and pushing through, no matter what. This lesson is as applicable today as it was in ancient Sparta. Whether facing a professional setback, personal loss, or a global

crisis, resilience is crucial to navigating challenges and emerging more robust on the other side.
- Discipline: The samurais of Japan epitomise the value of discipline in nurturing the warrior mindset. Their lives were governed by a strict code of conduct - Bushido - which required utmost discipline in every aspect of life. For us, too, discipline is the cornerstone of success. Whether sticking to a healthy lifestyle, consistently performing at work, or pursuing personal goals, discipline helps us stay the course and achieve our objectives.
- Courage: The Vikings showed us that courage is not about the absence of fear but rather the ability to face and forge ahead. It's about stepping out of our comfort zones, taking risks, and venturing into the unknown - something we can all apply in our personal and professional lives.
- Mindfulness: The Shaolin Monks of China demonstrate how mindfulness and spirituality can be intertwined with the warrior mindset. In today's fast-paced world, mindfulness has become more critical than ever. It helps us stay centred, focus on the present, and respond to situations with clarity rather than react impulsively.
- Community and Service: We learn the importance of community and service in the warrior ethos from indigenous cultures worldwide. It's a reminder that our actions impact those around us, and with the warrior mindset, we can contribute positively to our communities and society.

In conclusion, these historical and cultural examples of the warrior mindset provide invaluable lessons. They offer insights into values and practices that can help us face our modern-day challenges with courage, resilience, and wisdom.

Conclusion

As we reach the end of this enlightening journey through the annals of history and culture, it becomes undeniably clear that the warrior mindset is not a modern invention or a trendy buzzword. It is a timeless, universal ethos that has guided warriors across continents and epochs. It has been an integral part of cultures as diverse as the samurais of Japan, the Spartans of Ancient Greece, the Vikings of Scandinavia, the indigenous cultures around the world, and the Shaolin monks of China. Though the specifics vary from culture to culture, the core principles remain consistent. The warrior mindset embodies discipline, courage, resilience, mindfulness, and service. It's about harnessing our inner strength to conquer external and internal battles, navigate life's tumultuous seas with equanimity, and always strive to be a better version of ourselves. Each of these cultures gives us a different lens through which we can understand and incorporate the warrior mindset into our lives. They present to us an array of strategies that we can use to combat our daily struggles and challenges, both big and small. In today's fast-paced, unpredictable world, we often face circumstances demanding more from us than ever. In these moments, the warrior mindset can guide us, giving us the strength and resilience to face adversity, the courage to venture into the unknown, and the discipline to stay the course. It's an enduring ethos that encourages us to grow, evolve, and transcend our perceived limitations. So, as we close this chapter, let's carry forward the essence of these lessons. With its different cultural representations, the warrior mindset is a powerful tool for personal growth and success. It is not confined to extraordinary individuals or circumstances; it is accessible to all of us at every moment. In the spirit of the warriors we've met on this journey, let's embody their ethos, transform our mindset, and march forward with determination, resilience, and courage. The path of the warrior awaits. Let's take the first step.

Chapter 9

The Warrior Mindset in Times of Crisis

As we embark on this chapter, I want to focus on the crucial role of the warrior mindset in navigating crises. Crisis can strike in any form and at any time - personal loss, professional setbacks, health issues, financial troubles, natural disasters, global pandemics, the list is endless. No one is immune to experiencing crisis situations, but what truly matters is how we respond to them. The warrior mindset, as we've explored throughout this book, equips us with the resilience, courage, adaptability, and mental toughness needed to face these crises head-on. It prepares us to survive and find ways to thrive even amidst adversity. In this chapter, we'll delve deeper into how the warrior mindset acts as a beacon during tumultuous times. Through real-life examples and practical applications, we will see that crises are inherently challenging and offer us opportunities for profound personal growth and transformation when approached with a warrior mindset. We'll explore how the principles of the warrior mindset, such as emotional control, self-discipline, focused intention, resilience, and continuous growth, are not just theoretical concepts. They are powerful tools that can be honed and used to steer us through the stormy seas of crisis towards the calm waters of resolution and growth. By the end of this chapter, I hope you'll be equipped with the knowledge and confidence to face any crisis that comes your way with the strength of a warrior. Let's get started.

Defining Crisis

We must first understand what constitutes a crisis to navigate a crisis using the warrior mindset. At its core, a crisis is a significant, often sudden, disruption that threatens the stability of our lives or our sense of well-being. They are intense situations filled with uncertainty and stress.

Crises can manifest in many ways and on multiple scales. Let's explore three broad categories of crises:

1. **Personal crises:** These are profoundly individual and can encompass a wide range of situations, including health challenges like a severe diagnosis or mental health struggles, relationship problems such as a breakup or divorce, or personal loss, including the death of a loved one.
2. **Professional crises:** These could include job loss, career setbacks, or significant changes in your work environment. For an entrepreneur, it could be a business failure or substantial financial loss. For an employee, it could be unexpected redundancy or a problematic relationship with a boss or coworker.
3. **Broader societal crises:** These are large-scale events affecting entire communities, nations, or even the world. They can include economic downturns, natural disasters, or pandemics like the COVID-19 crisis. While they affect us as individuals, they also disrupt our broader societal structures, creating collective stress and hardship.

It's important to note that a minor issue for one person can be a full-blown crisis for another. The perception and impact of a crisis are highly individual, often depending on our personal circumstances, resilience, support network, and, importantly, our mindset.

The Role of the Warrior Mindset in Crisis

As we journey through life, we inevitably encounter crises. These moments test our strength and resolve, allowing us to grow and evolve. This is where the warrior mindset comes into play. It equips us with the mental and emotional tools to navigate crises effectively.

1. **Resilience**: One of the hallmarks of the warrior mindset is resilience – the ability to bounce back in the face of adversity. Crises will knock us down, but resilience allows us to rise, dust ourselves off, and forge ahead. It's not about avoiding falls but learning how to get up repeatedly.
2. **Adaptability**: Crises often involve sudden, unexpected changes. The warrior mindset helps us stay adaptable and ready to pivot and change. This quality can be crucial when navigating a crisis's unfamiliar terrain, helping us turn uncertainty into opportunity.
3. **Focus under Pressure**: In the heart of a crisis, fear and anxiety can threaten to overwhelm us. However, the warrior mindset teaches us to maintain focus amidst the chaos, honing our ability to stay grounded and clear-headed even under immense pressure.
4. **Finding Meaning in Adversity**: One of the most powerful aspects of the warrior mindset is the capacity to find meaning in adversity. Crises can be intensely painful and disorienting but also catalysts for profound personal growth and transformation. The warrior mindset helps us to frame our situations not merely as tragedies but as opportunities for learning and self-discovery.

Case Studies of Crisis Management

Let's delve into a couple of real-life case studies that illustrate the power of the warrior mindset in navigating crises.

Case Study 1 - The Life-Saving Decision:
In 2009, Captain Chesley "Sully" Sullenberger had to make a life-altering decision. Just minutes after his plane took off from New York's LaGuardia Airport, a flock of birds struck the engines, causing them to fail. With more than 150 lives at

stake and no time for indecision, Sullenberger remained calm, focused, and quickly decided to land the plane in the Hudson River. This event became known as the "Miracle on the Hudson." Sullenberger's resilience, focus under pressure and adaptability - all elements of the warrior mindset - saved the lives of everyone on board.

Case Study 2 - Turning Adversity into Advantage:
Consider the case of Airbnb, which was hit hard during the COVID-19 pandemic as global travel reached a standstill. Faced with a significant crisis, the company didn't fold under pressure. Instead, it displayed adaptability by swiftly pivoting its business model to offer online experiences and longer-term stays for people working from home. They found meaning in adversity and transformed their business to thrive in a difficult time. The warrior mindset principles of adaptability, resilience, and finding meaning in trouble were instrumental in successfully navigating the crisis.

These case studies underscore the transformative power of the warrior mindset when dealing with crises. The principles of resilience, adaptability, focus under pressure, and finding meaning in adversity are not only theoretical constructs; they have practical, real-world applications that can help us turn crisis into opportunity.

Practical Tips for Applying the Warrior Mindset in Times of Crisis

Applying the warrior mindset during a crisis may seem daunting. Still, with these practical tips and strategies, you can cultivate this mindset and adversity.

1. **Stay Focused:** In a crisis, it's easy to get overwhelmed by the sheer scale of the problem. However, maintaining focus on what you can control is essential. Prioritise

tasks, break them down into manageable chunks and tackle them one at a time.
2. **Practice Resilience:** Crises are inherently stressful, and feeling down is natural. But remember, the warrior mindset is about resilience. It's not about ignoring your emotions but acknowledging them and bouncing back. Exercise, meditation, and a healthy lifestyle can help build strength.
3. **Embrace Adaptability:** During a crisis, circumstances can change rapidly. Adaptability and flexibility in your thinking will allow you to navigate these changes and find innovative solutions to new problems.
4. **Finding Meaning in Adversity:** This can be the most challenging and transformative part. Try to find a lesson or opportunity for growth in the crisis. This can provide a sense of purpose and direction, helping you maintain a positive outlook.
5. **Reach Out to Your Support Network**: Warriors do not fight alone. Contact your friends, family, or professional networks for support and encouragement. Sometimes, knowing you're not alone can give you the strength to persist.
6. **Regular Mindfulness Practice:** Mindfulness can help you stay centred and focused amid chaos. Standard practice can involve formal meditation or taking a few minutes each day to be present and attentive to your surroundings and inner state of being.

By practising these strategies, you can cultivate the warrior mindset and enhance your ability to effectively navigate crises. Remember, like any skill, it takes time and practice to develop - so be patient with yourself.

Turning Crisis into Opportunity

As we venture deeper into the ethos of the warrior mindset, we come to one of its most potent and transformative aspects: the ability to turn crisis into opportunity. This is the most empowering facet of the warrior mindset - recognising that within every adversity lies the potential for growth and transformation. For many, a crisis represents an ending, a disruption to everyday life that is feared and avoided. However, for the warrior, a crisis is not merely a challenge to be overcome. It is an opportunity, a catalyst for personal and professional development. The Chinese word for crisis, 'weiji', comprises two characters: danger and opportunity. It beautifully captures this duality inherent in any crisis. How does the warrior mindset facilitate this shift in perception? It begins with acceptance. A warrior does not waste energy resisting what is already happening. They acknowledge the crisis, understanding that it is a part of life. This acceptance is not passive resignation but an active acknowledgement of reality, allowing for clear thinking and effective action. Next, the warrior leverages resilience and adaptability, staying flexible in the face of changing circumstances, bouncing back from setbacks, and being ready to seize new opportunities that arise from the upheaval. Perhaps most importantly, the warrior seeks to find meaning in the crisis. They ask, "What can I learn from this? How can this strengthen me? How can I improve?" This search for meaning can bring about profound personal growth and transformation. It can foster new skills, strengthen character, deepen empathy, and often lead to new paths that wouldn't have been discovered otherwise.

Consider the story of Thomas Edison. When his laboratory was destroyed by fire, he didn't despair. He reportedly said, "All our mistakes are burned up. Thank God we can start anew." And within three weeks, he had made a significant breakthrough in his work. In conclusion, through the lens of the warrior mindset, a crisis can be much more than a challenging problem. It can be a powerful catalyst for growth, change, and innovation, turning the seemingly worst of times into a unique opportunity for transformation. But remember, this process is not always easy, and it requires courage, persistence, and an unwavering commitment to growth – just like a warrior.

Summary and Key Takeaways

Throughout this chapter, we've delved deeply into the vital role the warrior mindset plays during times of crisis. Now, let's summarise the key points and distil some takeaways that can serve as guideposts on your journey to cultivating the warrior mindset:

1. **Defining Crisis:** A crisis can be personal, professional, or societal. From health challenges and job losses to global pandemics and economic downturns, a crisis is typically characterised by a significant disruption to everyday life.
2. **The Role of the Warrior Mindset in Crisis:** The warrior mindset equips individuals to effectively handle crises. It brings resilience, adaptability, focus under pressure, and a relentless quest for meaning in adversity.
3. **Real-life Case Studies:** We examined real-life cases where individuals and organisations have utilised the warrior mindset to navigate crises effectively. These stories are potent illustrations of how the principles of the warrior mindset can be applied in practice.
4. **Practical Tips:** We shared actionable strategies for applying the warrior mindset in times of crisis. These include accepting reality, fostering resilience and adaptability, maintaining focus under pressure, and actively seeking meaning and learning in adversity.

5. **Turning Crisis into Opportunity:** The warrior mindset can transform how we perceive and respond to crises. Rather than seeing them as challenges to overcome, warriors view crises as opportunities for growth and transformation.

Remember, the warrior mindset isn't an overnight transformation - it's a lifelong journey of growth and self-discovery. And as we have explored in this chapter, it's a powerful ally during times of crisis, helping you survive and thrive in adversity, turning challenges into opportunities for growth and transformation.

Conclusion

As we close this chapter, I want to reinforce the critical role of the warrior mindset in facing and overcoming crises. Life, as we all know, is not a linear journey. It is full of ups and downs, triumphs, and trials. And while we cannot control many of the challenges and crises that come our way, we do have a say in how we respond to them. The warrior mindset offers us a roadmap to turn adversity into an opportunity. It does not dismiss or diminish the hardships we face. Still, it empowers us to meet them head-on with courage, resilience, and adaptability. Through this lens, a crisis is not merely a stumbling block but a stepping stone - an opportunity to learn, grow, and transform. From personal adversities to professional setbacks to societal upheavals, the warrior mindset equips us to navigate the unpredictable terrain of crisis with steadiness and strength. It fosters resilience, cultivates focus, inspires adaptability, and urges us to find meaning and purpose amidst the chaos.

Remember the principles outlined in this chapter in the face of a crisis. Apply the strategies, draw inspiration from the case studies, and always take advantage of the opportunity in every challenge. Being a warrior is not about invulnerability but confronting vulnerability and transforming it into strength. It's about standing firm during the storm, not because you're impervious to the winds, but because you've cultivated an unwavering belief in your ability to endure, adapt, and ultimately thrive. And remember, the warrior's journey is continuous, and each crisis faced and conquered strengthens your warrior spirit. The road may be rough, the journey challenging, but armed with the warrior mindset, there is no adversity you cannot turn into an opportunity. Keep walking the path of the warrior. In the face of crisis, stand tall, stand firm, and remember - you have the heart of a warrior.

Chapter 10
Practical Techniques for Cultivating the Warrior Mindset

As we begin this next chapter, it is time to focus on the practical, actionable steps you can take to cultivate your warrior mindset. Throughout this journey, we've delved deep into the philosophy, the principles, and the profound impact of the warrior mindset. We've seen it through the lens of history, case studies, and real-life applications in the throes of crises and everyday life. Now, it's time to transition from understanding to action. Mindset, after all, is not just about thinking - it's also about doing. It's about translating those beliefs and attitudes into tangible actions. In this chapter, we will be focusing on just that. We're going to explore a set of practical techniques you can use to foster and strengthen your warrior mindset. Remember, embarking on the warrior's path is not a passive endeavour. It requires active participation. It's not enough to simply know the tenets of the warrior mindset; one must put them into practice. It's a dynamic process, an interplay of knowledge, awareness, and action. In the words of Bruce Lee, "Knowing is not enough. We must apply. Willing is not enough. We must do." This chapter is about application and action. It's about equipping you with the tools you need to manifest the warrior mindset in your day-to-day life, guiding you as you turn philosophy into practice.

Mindfulness Techniques

Mindfulness forms a core pillar of the warrior mindset. It is the ability to be fully present, aware of where we are and what we're doing, and not overly reactive or overwhelmed by what's happening around us. And just like any other skill, mindfulness can be trained and cultivated with regular practice.

1. **Mindfulness Meditation**: This is a fundamental practice in cultivating mindfulness. Sit comfortably, with your back straight, and focus on your breath. When your

mind wanders (and it will), gently bring it back to the breath. Start with just a few minutes daily, then gradually increase the time as your comfort and concentration improve.
2. **Mindful Eating**: We often eat mindlessly in front of our computers or TVs, not really paying attention to the taste, texture, or the act of eating itself. Try making at least one meal a day a mindful one. Sit down, remove distractions, and focus on the food. Smell it, taste it, and savour each bite.
3. **Mindfulness-based Stress Reduction (MBSR)**: Developed by Jon Kabat-Zinn, MBSR is an eight-week program that involves mindfulness meditation, body awareness, and mindful movement (like yoga) to help reduce stress and improve mental and physical health. Many resources are available online if you wish to follow this structured approach.
4. **Mindful Walking**: This is simply choosing to be aware as you walk. Feel the ground beneath your feet, notice the wind against your skin, the sounds around you. It's a great way to incorporate mindfulness into your daily routine.
5. **Mindful Breathing**: Whether waiting for a meeting to start or sitting in traffic, you can always practice mindful breathing. Focus on your breath, and observe it flowing in and out. It's a simple yet powerful way to ground yourself in the present moment.

Incorporating these techniques into your daily routine can significantly enhance your sense of presence, a vital aspect of the warrior mindset. These practices allow us to maintain our focus on the present, grounding us in the here and now and providing us with the clarity and serenity necessary to face life's challenges head-on.

Cognitive Restructuring Techniques

Cognitive restructuring is a psychological technique that helps you to identify, challenge and alter stress-inducing thought patterns and beliefs. We can improve our emotions, behaviours, and lives by changing our thoughts. Here are some specific cognitive restructuring techniques:

1. **Thought-stopping**: This technique involves interrupting, stopping, and changing negative thoughts that may be overwhelming. When a negative thought enters your mind, you consciously issue a command, like "Stop!" to interrupt the pattern. Then, you redirect your attention to something positive or neutral.
2. **Thought substitution**: Instead of merely trying to suppress a negative thought (which often backfires), thought substitution involves replacing negative thinking with a more positive one. For example, if the thought "I'm terrible at this" arises, you might replace it with "I'm learning and improving."
3. **Use of affirmations**: Affirmations are positive statements that can help you to challenge and overcome self-sabotaging and negative thoughts. When you repeat them often and believe in them, you can start to make positive changes. An affirmation could be as simple as "I am capable and strong" or, more specifically, "I have all the resources I need to tackle this challenge."
4. **Cognitive reframing:** This involves changing your perspective on a negative situation or experience in a way that is neither false nor harmful but positive and empowering. For example, viewing a failure as a learning opportunity.
5. **Journaling**: Writing out thoughts and worries can help identify negative thinking patterns. After identifying these thoughts, you can work on challenging them and replacing them with more positive, realistic thoughts.

These techniques can be powerful tools in cultivating the warrior mindset. By training ourselves to identify and challenge our negative thought patterns, we can foster a more resilient, adaptive, and prepared mindset to face the challenges that come our way.

Physical Practices

The warrior mindset isn't solely about mental and emotional strength; physical practices also play a pivotal role. Physical training and techniques provide an essential foundation that supports and enhances our cognitive abilities. The discipline, resilience, and focus that comes from physical activity can significantly contribute to cultivating the warrior mindset.

1. **Regular Exercise:** A consistent exercise routine, whether running, cycling, weight training, or any other form of physical activity, can strengthen our resolve and discipline. Exercise also boosts our mood and mental health, contributing to a stronger warrior mindset.
2. **Martial Arts:** Martial arts training is more than just physical conditioning; it also involves cultivating the mind and spirit. Many martial arts, such as Karate, Taekwondo, Brazilian Jiu-Jitsu, and Kung Fu, emphasise mental discipline, respect, patience, and a strong will. These elements align closely with the principles of the warrior mindset.
3. **Yoga and Tai Chi:** Practices like Yoga and Tai Chi combine physical postures, breathing exercises, and meditation. They promote physical strength and flexibility, mental calm, focus, and awareness, essential elements of the warrior mindset.
4. **Outdoor Activities:** Activities like hiking, rock climbing, or even gardening can help connect us with nature and provide a sense of peace and

groundedness. They also present challenges that require mental strength and resilience to overcome.
5. **Mindful Movement:** This involves bringing a sense of mindfulness to any physical activity, paying close attention to what you're feeling in your body and the world around you. This could apply to walking, dancing, or any other movement-based activity.

Remember, these physical practices aim to enhance our physical fitness and cultivate a warrior mindset. It's about developing mental toughness, discipline, focus, and resilience. It's about becoming a stronger, more capable version of ourselves physically, mentally, and emotionally.

Journaling and Reflection

An essential part of cultivating the warrior mindset is developing a solid self-awareness, and understanding is critical to growing the warrior mindset. A potent tool to foster this self-awareness and promote growth is the practice of journaling and reflection.

1. **Journaling:** is a powerful practice to clear your mind and articulate your thoughts, emotions, and experiences. Journaling can help you track your progress, reflect on your experiences, and gain insights into your behaviours and patterns. It can become a medium to converse with yourself, helping you better understand your strengths, weaknesses, fears, and aspirations.
2. **Types of Journaling:** There are many ways to journal. You could maintain a gratitude journal listing things you're grateful for daily. Or it could be a goal journal where you articulate your goals, strategies, and progress. A dream journal could help you understand your subconscious mind better. Experiment with different types and find what resonates most with you.

3. **Reflection:** Alongside journaling, taking time out of your day for reflection is vital. Reflect on your actions, decisions, and experiences. Try to understand why you behaved in a certain way or why certain things affect you as they do. Reflection fosters self-awareness, which is crucial in developing the warrior mindset.
4. **Meditation and Mindfulness:** These practices go hand in hand with reflection. They encourage you to be present and attentive to your thoughts and feelings without judgment. Over time, this heightened self-awareness and understanding can help you navigate your life with more wisdom and grace, the hallmarks of the warrior mindset.

Remember, the warrior mindset requires a deep understanding of self. Practices like journaling and reflection can help you understand your motivations, fears, strengths, and areas for improvement. By understanding yourself better, you can train and harness your mind more effectively, just as a true warrior would.

Visualisation Techniques

Visualisation is a potent tool in the cultivation of the warrior mindset. It involves creating a mental image or intention of what you desire to happen or feel. This mental rehearsal primes your brain and body to act in ways that align with your imagined scenario, effectively training you for the event in your mind before it happens in reality. Here's how you can incorporate visualisation techniques into your life:

1. **Goal Visualization**: Start by visualising your goals. See yourself achieving these goals in as much detail as possible. Feel the sense of satisfaction, pride, and emotions you'd experience once you reach your goal. This technique has been used by many successful people, from athletes to entrepreneurs, to keep their

goals front and centre in their minds and their motivation levels high.
2. **Process Visualisation**: While visualising the end goal is helpful, visualising the process is equally important. This means imagining yourself taking the steps needed to reach your goal. See yourself facing challenges and overcoming them. This visualisation can help you prepare for obstacles and cultivate the resilience necessary to overcome adversity.
3. **Relaxation Visualisation**: Use visualisation to reduce stress and increase feelings of calm. Picture yourself in a peaceful setting, like a beach or a forest. Engage all your senses in this visualisation - feel the wind on your skin, hear the sound of the waves or the rustling leaves, smell the ocean or the trees. This technique can be a quick way to tap into a more relaxed state of mind.
4. **Performance Visualisation**: This is particularly useful if you're preparing for a specific event - a job interview, a public speech, or a sports competition. Visualise yourself performing perfectly and confidently. Feel the positivity and the rush of doing well.

The key to effective visualisation is consistency and detail. The more vivid your visualisation, the more your brain will register the image as reality. Regularly practising these visualisation techniques will help you cultivate a focused, resilient warrior mindset, preparing you for future success.

Creating a Warrior Mindset Routine

To cultivate the warrior mindset, we must move beyond understanding its principles and actively integrate these concepts into our daily lives. This means setting up a warrior mindset routine, a daily or weekly activity regimen reinforcing our discussed principles. Consistency, after all, is critical. The more regularly you engage with these practices, the more they become second nature. Here's a guide to help you create your warrior mindset routine:

1. **Establish a Mindfulness Practice:** Begin each day with a mindfulness exercise. This could be as simple as spending 5-10 minutes daily in mindful meditation. Sit quietly, focus on your breath, and when your mind wanders (as it inevitably will), gently bring your attention back to the present moment. This practice will help you start your day with a clear, focused mind.
2. **Set Your Intentions**: Post-meditation, set your intentions for the day. What do you want to accomplish? How do you want to feel? Visualise yourself achieving your goals and the steps you'll need to take to get there.
3. **Engage in Physical Activity**: Physical practices are essential to cultivating the warrior mindset. Make time each day for some form of exercise, whether a vigorous workout, a martial arts class, or a simple walk in nature. This not only strengthens your body but also your mind, enhancing your focus and resilience.
4. **Practice Cognitive Restructuring**: When faced with challenges or stressful situations, take a moment to practice cognitive restructuring. Challenge any negative thoughts, and replace them with positive, empowering ones. This process can be facilitated by maintaining a thought journal where you write down negative thoughts and actively work on reframing them.
5. **Reflect and Journal**: End each day with a reflection. Write in your journal about your experiences, challenges, and how you applied the warrior mindset to deal with them. This practice promotes self-awareness and helps you see your growth over time.
6. **Visualise Success**: Before going to bed, visualise your success. See yourself achieving your goals, overcoming obstacles, and becoming the warrior you aspire to be.

This sets a positive tone for the following day but also aids in cultivating a mindset of success.

Remember, the goal of this routine isn't to add more tasks to your day but to help you align your daily actions with the principles of the warrior mindset. Adjust this routine to fit your lifestyle and needs, but keep the core components intact. The warrior mindset is all about adaptability, resilience, and focus. These practices will help you strengthen these attributes and ultimately transform you into the warrior you're destined to be.

Conclusion

Cultivating the warrior mindset isn't a quick fix or a magic bullet - it is a continuous journey of self-growth, discipline, and resilience. Each step forward is a testament to your strength and commitment to personal development. It's a transformative process, a gradual shift from reacting to life's challenges to proactively taking charge and shaping your life with intent and purpose.

Patience and perseverance are vital elements of this journey. Changes in mindset do not occur overnight. They are the product of consistent practice and a deep commitment to personal growth. But remember, every small step forward counts. Every time you choose to engage in mindfulness, every moment you challenge a negative thought, and each day you decide to engage in physical activity, you're solidifying your warrior mindset. Take pride in your progress, no matter how small it might seem. These little victories are the building blocks of your warrior mindset, the foundation for strength, resilience, and focus. They are proof of your determination, your tenacity, and your willpower. In closing, remember this: cultivating a warrior mindset is not always easy, but it is undoubtedly worthwhile. The challenges you face along the way are not barriers but stepping stones on your path to becoming a warrior. With the warrior mindset, there are no losses, lessons, failures, or opportunities for growth. Keep this in mind as you continue your journey. Hold onto the warrior spirit. Nurture it. Live it. You're on the path to becoming a true warrior, and each step you take brings you closer to becoming the most potent, most resilient version of yourself. Remember, the warrior's journey is lifelong, but you're growing more robust, resilient, and focused each day. Embrace the journey, for it shapes you into the warrior you are destined to be.

Chapter 11

The Journey Ahead

Becoming a Warrior

As we open this final chapter of our journey, let's take a moment to look back on the ground we've covered together. You've come a long way since the start of this book, diving into the depths of what it means to adopt the warrior mindset. We've explored the philosophical underpinnings of this mindset, dissected its key components, drawn inspiration from historical and modern-day warriors, and delved into practical techniques for cultivating this mindset in our everyday lives. Throughout this journey, you've engaged with various concepts, principles, and practices - all essential elements of the warrior mindset. From the pillars of focus, discipline, and resilience to the values of honour, integrity, and service, we've seen how these principles shape the mindset of a warrior. We've also examined how the warrior mindset stands as a beacon of strength and adaptability during times of crisis, turning adversities into opportunities for growth.

Moreover, we've journeyed together through real-life stories that showcased the warrior mindset in action, offering tangible proof of its transformative power. These stories served as a testament to the incredible potential that this mindset unlocks, whether in personal development, professional growth, or societal change. Lastly, we took a hands-on approach, diving into practical techniques to nurture the warrior mindset. Mindfulness, cognitive restructuring, physical practices, journaling, and visualisation are the tools at your disposal to carve out the warrior's path. The journey so far has been insightful, empowering, and transformative. But it's essential to remember that this journey doesn't end as we turn the final pages of this book. Instead, it begins a lifelong commitment to growth, resilience, and continuous self-improvement. So, as we move forward, let's reflect on the lessons learned and the road ahead. Let's explore what it truly means to become a warrior.

Continuous Learning and Growth

The warrior mindset is not a destination; it's a journey of continuous learning, growth, and transformation. It's an ongoing commitment to nurturing the best within you, pushing your boundaries, and striving to rise above your past self. It's not about reaching a static endpoint but about evolving, growing, and transforming throughout your life. The idea of Kaizen, a Japanese concept meaning "continuous improvement," embodies this aspect of the warrior mindset. It's about taking small, consistent steps towards personal, professional, or societal improvement. Whether it's honing your skills, broadening your knowledge, improving your health, or nurturing your relationships, the key lies in maintaining an ongoing commitment to learning and growth. A growth mindset, a concept popularised by psychologist Carol Dweck, is vital to this journey. It involves seeing challenges as opportunities for growth, viewing failures as learning experiences, and understanding that abilities and intelligence can be developed. It's about believing in your capacity to learn, change, and grow over time. As a warrior, you must foster curiosity, openness, and a love for learning. Stay informed about the world, embrace new experiences, and never stop learning from them. Immerse yourself in books, engage in stimulating conversations, and seek out mentors and teachers who can guide you on your journey. Moreover, the warrior's path is also about inner growth-developing emotional intelligence, cultivating mindfulness, nurturing resilience, and fostering a strong sense of purpose. It's about introspection and self-reflection, understanding your strengths and weaknesses, and constantly striving to become the best version of yourself. So remember, becoming a warrior isn't a one-time accomplishment-it's a lifelong pursuit. It's about embodying the principles of the warrior mindset each day, learning from every experience, and continuously striving to grow, improve, and transform. As Bruce Lee famously said, "There are no limits. There are only plateaus, and you must not stay there. You must go beyond them." So, keep pushing your limits, climbing those plateaus, and continuing your journey towards becoming a true warrior.

Overcoming Future Challenges

As a warrior, you have invaluable tools to navigate life's ups and downs. You've learned that the warrior mindset isn't only about overcoming adversity; it's also about leveraging it as a catalyst for growth, transformation, and personal breakthroughs. Life is inherently unpredictable and filled with challenges. There will be times of joy, success but also times of struggle, failure, and pain. Yet, as you've discovered, it's not the external circumstances that define you but your response to them. It's about how you navigate through these challenges, how you rise after a fall, and how you learn from each experience. Here's where the principles and techniques of the warrior mindset come into play. They are your compass during adversity, your anchor in a stormy sea. They allow you to remain focused, resilient, and adaptable, no matter your challenges. When you meet a personal setback, tap into your resilience, maintain your focus, and view the situation as an opportunity to learn and grow. If you encounter a professional obstacle, leverage your adaptability, and find creative solutions. If you confront a societal crisis, utilise your warrior ethos to contribute positively to your community. Remember the techniques you've learned-mindfulness, cognitive restructuring, physical practices, journaling, visualisation, and routine building. These are your tools for navigating life's challenges and honing your warrior mindset. Above all, remember that every challenge is an opportunity in disguise. It's a chance to put your warrior mindset to the test, to learn, to grow, and to come out stronger on the other side. As the philosopher Friedrich Nietzsche once said, "That which does not kill us makes us stronger." So face your future challenges with courage, confidence, and the heart of a warrior. You are not just a survivor but a thriver, ready to turn every adversity into an advantage.

A Lifelong Commitment

Adopting the warrior mindset is not a temporary endeavour or a short-term project. Instead, it's a lifelong commitment, a continuous journey of growth, self-improvement, and personal evolution. Embracing the warrior mindset is about far more than learning a set of techniques or adopting a new perspective. It's about fundamentally reshaping your identity, redefining your life approach, and transforming your interactions with the world. It's about becoming a warrior in thought, action, spirit, and being. This mindset becomes deeply integrated into your life, influencing your decisions, shaping your responses, and guiding your efforts. It's there when you face adversity, reminding you to be resilient and adaptable. It's there when you set goals, urging you to stay focused and disciplined. It's there when you interact with others, inspiring you to act with honour, respect, and service. Yet, like any other aspect of your identity, your warrior mindset can grow and evolve. As you face new experiences and challenges and learn and grow, your understanding and embodiment of the warrior mindset deepen. It's an ongoing process of exploration, reflection, and refinement. You may start by consciously applying the warrior mindset principles in certain situations. Yet, these principles become intrinsic to your thought patterns, behaviour, and character. They become second nature, an integral part of who you are. Embracing the warrior mindset is thus a profound journey of personal transformation. It's a path that requires courage, commitment, and continuous effort. Yet, the rewards are immense. A warrior mindset equips you to lead a life of purpose, resilience, and fulfilment. It enables you to not just survive life's battles and thrive and grow from them, emerging as a more robust, wiser, and more empowered individual. Remember, the journey to becoming a warrior is not a destination-it's the path itself. So keep walking this path with dedication, resilience, and the heart of a warrior. As you do, you'll discover the true power of the warrior mindset and the extraordinary potential within you.

Building a Warrior Community

Embarking to cultivate a warrior mindset is a deeply personal endeavour. It requires introspection, self-reflection, and individual determination. However, that does not mean you have to, or should, undertake this journey alone. Humans are inherently social creatures, and we often find strength, motivation, and insight through interactions. This is why building or joining a community of like-minded individuals can be incredibly beneficial as you strive to develop and deepen your warrior mindset. These could be people who share your commitment to personal growth and resilience and mindfulness-fellow warriors on their own path of self-improvement and transformation. Such a community provides a supportive environment that can enhance your warrior journey in several ways:

1. **Mutual Support:** Life's challenges can sometimes be daunting. Having a supportive community provides a sense of solidarity. Knowing that others are facing similar struggles can be comforting and empowering. You can lean on each other for support, encouragement, and motivation.

2. **Shared Learning:** Everyone's journey is unique and has its own insights and experiences. By sharing these, everyone in the community can learn and grow together. You can glean insights from others' experiences, learn from their successes and failures, and gain new perspectives.
3. **Accountability:** Making a commitment to ourselves can sometimes be easy to break. However, when we commit to others, we're more likely to stick to them. Being part of a community can provide that sense of accountability. Your fellow warriors can help keep you on track, gently reminding you of your commitment to the warrior mindset when you stumble.
4. **Collective Growth:** There is a unique power in collective growth and transformation. As each individual in the community grows and evolves, the entire group benefits. You can inspire and be inspired, motivate and be motivated, teach and be taught.

Building or finding your warrior community can happen in many ways. It could start online through social media groups or forums dedicated to personal growth and resilience. Or it could be more local, like a book club, a meditation group, or a fitness class in your neighbourhood. It could be as simple as starting a regular discussion with a group of close friends, all dedicated to supporting each other's growth. Remember, the journey towards the warrior mindset is not one you need to make alone. By finding or creating a community of fellow warriors, you can enhance your growth, find support and camaraderie, and collectively embody the principles of the warrior mindset. In doing so, you'll not just transform your own life but also contribute to the growth and transformation of others.

Sharing the Warrior Mindset

As you deepen your understanding and application of the warrior mindset, you will naturally begin to embody its principles: resilience, focus, adaptability, and a deep sense of purpose. People around you will likely notice this change. They'll see your enhanced ability to handle stress, your unwavering focus on your goals, and your capacity to turn challenges into opportunities for growth. In this way, you become a living example of the power of the warrior mindset. But embodying the warrior mindset is just the first step. The next is to share it, to inspire others in your life to cultivate these qualities within themselves. Here's how you can do it:

1. **Model the Warrior Mindset**: Your actions often speak louder than words. By modelling the warrior mindset daily, you can subtly encourage others to adopt similar attitudes and behaviours. When they see you facing adversity with resilience, staying focused amidst distractions, and continuously striving for personal growth, they'll be inspired to do the same.
2. **Encourage Others**: Whenever you see someone facing a challenge, remind them of the warrior within them. Encourage them to meet their challenges head-on, embrace change and uncertainty as opportunities for growth, and stay focused on their goals no matter what distractions come.
3. **Teach the Principles**: Share your knowledge about the warrior mindset with others. This could be as simple as recommending books or resources that have helped you or as involved as mentoring someone on their own journey to cultivate the warrior mindset.
4. **Promote Mindfulness**: Encourage those around you to practice mindfulness. This could be as simple as suggesting they take a few minutes daily to breathe and

focus on the present. Alternatively, it could involve inviting them to join you in a yoga or meditation class.
5. **Create or Join a Community**: Building a warrior community can benefit you and everyone involved. Invite others to join you in this community, creating a space for mutual support, shared learning, and collective growth.
6. **Be Patient and Compassionate**: Everyone is on their own journey and will embrace the warrior mindset at their own pace. Some might be resistant or sceptical at first. Be patient with them, offering support and encouragement without pushing too hard. Above all, lead with compassion, understanding, and respect.

Sharing the warrior mindset with others helps them and reinforces your commitment to these principles. It keeps you accountable and deepens your understanding of the warrior mindset. And in the process, you'll contribute to a more resilient, mindful, and adaptable world-one warrior at a time.

Closing Remarks

Congratulations! You have embarked on a journey of transformation and self-discovery. This journey is not just about overcoming challenges, achieving external success, and embracing the warrior within you. In the face of adversity, resilient warriors stay focused on their path, adapt to change gracefully and find deep meaning and purpose in their lives. Each chapter, each principle, and each technique you've learned in this book is a stepping stone towards embodying the warrior mindset. It's important to remember that this journey is not a race or a competition. It is a path of personal growth and self-mastery. Some days, it might feel like you're leaping forward; others, it might feel like you're barely moving. But no matter how fast or slow you go, every step is in the right direction. Practising the warrior mindset will require patience, dedication, and, at times, courage. There will be challenges along the way and moments of self-doubt. But remember, it is through facing these challenges that you truly grow as a warrior. As you overcome each obstacle, you'll become stronger, more resilient, and more in tune with your true potential. Remember, the warrior mindset is not about being perfect. It's about striving for progress. It's about learning from your mistakes, adapting to changes, and continually moving forward. It's about realising that the power to shape your life lies within you. So, as you close this book, remember that this is not the end of your journey but just the beginning.

The principles and techniques you've learned are tools you can carry throughout your life. Use them wisely and consistently, and watch as they transform your life. Lastly, I encourage you to share what you've learned with others. The world needs more warriors. People who are resilient, mindful, adaptable, and purpose-driven. People like you. Here's to the journey ahead. To your journey. Your journey to becoming a warrior. Keep moving forward, keep growing, and never stop believing in the warrior within you. Your warrior journey has just begun. I look forward to seeing where it takes you. Congratulations, warrior. The journey continues. The warrior journey is yours.

Conclusion

And so, we come to the end of this book, but the beginning of your journey in cultivating the warrior mindset. Throughout these chapters, we've explored what it means to be a warrior in today's world. It's not about physical battles but the battles we face within ourselves - the battles of doubt, fear, complacency, and disconnection. We've uncovered the principles that define the warrior mindset - resilience, adaptability, focus, and purpose. These are not abstract concepts but concrete tools that can guide your everyday actions and decisions. By embracing these principles, you can face life's challenges with courage and poise, navigate change with agility, maintain focus amid distractions, and find deep meaning and fulfilment in your life's work. This book has presented case studies of people from different walks of life who've embodied the warrior mindset uniquely. Their stories serve as an inspiration and a reminder that the warrior mindset is not confined to any one field or endeavour. It's applicable whether you're an athlete pushing your physical limits, an entrepreneur creating value in the marketplace, an individual dealing with personal adversity, or an activist striving for social change. We've also delved into the practical side of cultivating the warrior mindset. Through mindfulness practices, cognitive restructuring techniques, physical disciplines, journaling, visualisation, and creating a warrior routine, you've been given a toolkit to help you integrate the warrior mindset into your daily life. It's important to remember that cultivating the warrior mindset is not an overnight transformation. It's a journey that requires patience, perseverance, and a commitment to lifelong learning.

You won't always get it right, and that's okay. It's not about perfection but progress. Each day offers a new opportunity to grow, learn, and step closer to the warrior you aspire to be. Remember, you're not alone in this journey. I encourage you to build your tribe of fellow warriors committed to this path of growth and self-mastery. You can support, learn from, and inspire each other to greater heights. As you close this book, I want you to realise that the warrior journey is now yours. You have the tools, the principles, and the inspiration to cultivate the warrior mindset. It's now up to you to put them into practice, to make them a part of your life, and to become the warrior you are capable of being. Embrace the journey ahead with courage, enthusiasm, and an open heart. You are stronger than you think. You are more capable than you believe. You are a warrior. Now, it's time to unleash your warrior spirit. Here's to your journey, warrior. May it be filled with growth, adventure, and abundant success. Go forth and conquer your world. Because the world needs more warriors, warriors like you.

Afterword or Acknowledgments

Firstly, I extend my heartfelt gratitude to everyone who has helped me become who I am today and made me what I am. Your support, feedback, and continuous encouragement have been invaluable.

I began this writing journey with a simple goal: write a book and help people. The journey, while challenging, has been one of immense growth and learning. Each word penned in this book represents my understanding and admiration for the warrior mindset. I sincerely hope it resonates with you, the reader, and inspires you to embrace your inner warrior.